# True stories of how past-life experiences hold the key to the mysteries of our lives today . . .

A white college professor who specialized in Black Studies frequently awoke from a nightmare in which he was choking on sand. The dreams were so real that he would actually be choking when he awoke. One day he attended a lecture in which Alex Haley told of how Africans kidnapped by the slave traders, bound and left on the beaches waiting to board slave ships, would commit suicide by deliberately swallowing sand. The professor instantly realized that his nightmare was recalling a powerful image from a past life.

Michael Parks was afraid of the dark; *deathly* afraid, to the point of suffocating if left in the dark too long. This fear dominated his life until a series of past-life recall exercises revealed that he had been left to die in the bottom of a well-like dungeon in a previous incarnation during the reign of Louis XIV of France.

Learn more about how *your* past lives may be affecting you right now in
**REINCARNATION.**

# REINCARNATION
## Your Secret Life

## John Van Auken

BALLANTINE BOOKS • NEW YORK

ISBN 0-345-35559-8

Manufactured in the United States of America

First Edition: April 1991

# Contents

**PART ONE: The Foundations of Reincarnation**

1. The Bittersweet Mysteries of Life   3
2. The Secret Genesis   15
3. A Stellar Dimension   29
4. The Physical Body   34
5. To The Rescue!   43
6. The Lives of Leila: One Soul's Journey   57

**PART TWO: Reincarnation Today**

7. Past Lives and Present Relationships   87
8. Destiny, Fate, and Karma   110
9. Past-Life Memory   120
10. The Power of an Ideal   144
11. Meditation: Tool for Transformation   151
12. Contact Dreams   163
13. Closing Thoughts   169

*Appendix One:* About Edgar Cayce   173
*Appendix Two:* Reincarnation and Christianity   177
*Recommended Reading*   181

# PART ONE

## The Foundations of Reincarnation

# 1

# The Bittersweet Mysteries of Life

ALL OF US have, at one time or another, struggled with questions about the meaning of life. Questions like: Why do we exist? Why are we born in this particular time and place? Is there a purpose to fulfill in life, a destiny to follow? Is there any rhyme or reason behind the events we experience or see around us? For example, why is one child born handicapped or into poverty, disease, oppression, and an early death, while another is born into comfort, opportunity, and a long, healthy life? Every day we hear news reports of an innocent person who has been brutally victimized by a total stranger, and we wonder how there could possibly be any sense to it. In some parts of the world people are starving, while in others people struggle to eat less and stay thin. One person takes a risk and makes a fortune while another loses everything.

Another of life's puzzles is why some of us seem to be born with a specific talent. How could Mozart, at nine years of age, write a symphony as well or better than people who have studied music all their lives? Where did his ability come from? Was Mozart simply *born* with it? Why? If so, are people chosen? Is there some understandable plan to our lives? Or, is it all the result of unpredictable forces of Nature, a great big game of chance?

Why do we strive so hard to learn, to achieve, to find and maintain love and friendships, to understand why we are here, only to die and be separated from it all; or worse yet, to simply cease to exist? Indeed, life is a mystery. And yet, something within us drives us to find purpose and meaning in it and to discover the answers to at least some of these questions.

In the Western world two dominant sources provide us with information: science and religion. Both try to unravel the mysteries of life. Both try to provide answers to help explain the nature of and purpose for our existence. To a limited extent they even try to explain the causes behind the circumstances of our lives—why it is the way it is, why some of us succeed and some fail, why some suffer and others go merrily along.

For the most part, science is a branch of knowledge that has been built on observable phenomena that can be substantiated by tests. Because it is centered around the observable universe, science relies on the perceptive powers of the five senses and the enhancement of these with instruments. Beyond sensually observed phenomena, it classifies most everything as theory. Therefore, reality, according to science, is what has been observed and can be substantiated through physical tests.

The driving force behind science is the pursuit of knowledge. Through investigation, study, hypotheses, and testing, knowledge of all things can be obtained. With knowledge will come understanding, and with enough knowledge the mystery can be solved.

Religion is quite different.

Religious ideas have been built on centuries of human beliefs, feelings, thoughts, and tenets that do not need to be observed by the senses or substantiated by tests. They are considered true because a significant number of the religion's adherents believe in them or because a great teacher has said so. In most cases the validity of the leader's teachings and the tenets of the followers are accepted as true because they are believed to have been divinely inspired.

The driving force behind religion is not knowledge; in fact, knowledge is seen as one of the causes of "original sin." For religion, faith is what binds the pieces of the puzzle together and lifts the veil of mystery from life. The faithful, it is said, will eventually know the truth.

Where science seeks knowledge, religion seeks faithfulness to the tenets. Where science gains through investigation, religion gains through living the tenets, and in some cases through inspiration and revelation. Where science uses reason and observation to identify truth, religion uses emotion and miraculous signs to indicate the presence of truth.

To begin our search to uncover the secrets of life, let's take a closer look at the major concepts found in science and religion and see what they reveal.

## The Observations of Science

Science predominantly defines life in biological terms. Something is "alive" if it manifests certain biological conditions, namely: growth through metabolism, the ability to adapt to its environment through changes originating internally, and the ability to reproduce itself. By this definition a rock is not alive and an amoeba is.

Added to the biological quality of being alive, science observes levels of "aliveness"—an amoeba may well be alive, but its level of awareness or consciousness in no way compares with that of a monkey. The monkey is more alive because it is not only biologically living through metabolism, reproduction, and internally adjusting adaptation, but it is also *perceiving* more of its inner and outer environment. It displays the conditions of having attitudes, emotions, and memories, as well as the powers of thinking, learning, and communicating.

When science looks around the observable world it sees gradations of "aliveness" from the merely biological to the highly conscious forms of life, and it sees evidence that these gradations have *evolved* over eons from the simple to the complex. Scientists have found enough evidence for them to propose that the origin of human life was a fortuitous event in the waters of this planet millions of years ago, in which circumstances were just right for the emergence of biological life in its simplest form. This basic life-form has evolved to the complex level we possess today.

At present, the scientific viewpoint, though contributing to the overall picture of the processes involved in life, does not give much meaning to us as individuals. Science observes the apparent purpose for life to be the perfection of the species through "survival of the fittest." Since one's life is determined by genetic structure and physical environment, the circumstances in one's life are a result of the forces of Nature.

An individual seeking answers, reasons, and meaning finds that life can be scientifically described as little more than the result of the random contact of one sperm cell with one egg, and the subsequent division of these cells, following a unique genetic code. This group of cells, now forming a body, will live approximately seventy to eighty years if it isn't destroyed by disease or some unfortunate incident, and will then stop living. It will cease to exist. Death is the end of life. Our species will go on perfecting the life-form through the genes passed on, but the parent body is no more. New beings will rise up, live in their glory, pass on their genes, and then decay and die.

Science has made great strides in prolonging life by the successful treatment of many diseases and through the use of artificial organs and other transplant procedures. As they find ways to extend our life span, more and more reports are surfacing of patients who have died on the operating table only to be brought back to life and consciousness, bringing with them stories of some sort of survival beyond physical death. Today, there are also many medical professionals who work quietly with healers and psychic diagnosticians and who have begun to view life and health as something more than just a biological phenomenon. The study of dreams, a much more respected undertaking today than it was even ten years ago, is telling us new things about who we are. Other medical professionals who are involved in the area of emotional healing are using controversial techniques of past-life regression, in which a patient is guided through experiences

from previous lifetimes in order to treat present phobias
-and other problems. With all of this, science has not yet
altered its position on the origin of or purpose for life, and
we are still left with many unanswered questions. So far,
no single idea, experience, or event has pushed the scientific core to change its methods and conclusions, but
each new bit of information provides a stepping stone toward what may be the dawn of a new science.

## Religion: A Leap of Faith

Religion, specifically Western, Judeo-Christian religion,
teaches that all life was created by a divine being, and that
although mysterious for man to understand, the creator's
ways are purposeful and have meaning.

In such a religious belief structure, man is God's greatest
creation. The individual human being is more than a biological organism; it is a "soul" or "spirit" that lives beyond biological death. From this view, life does not end,
and all the achievements, joys, loves, and memories are not
lost but contribute to the individual's existence beyond
death. Accordingly, man has the opportunity to live forever
with God in heaven after his or her earthly life.

Religion also provides explanations for suffering and misfortune, which can be outlined as follows.

Original sin was one of disobedience committed by man's
ancestors, Adam and Eve. They were the first man and
woman to be created and from whom all others have come.
These two lived with God in the Garden of Eden and walked
with him daily. But they ate a forbidden fruit from "the tree

of the knowledge of good and evil,'' and for this offense they were banished from the garden and the company of God. Consequently, life on earth is far from what it might have been.

The second reason for suffering and disappointment is misuse of one's ''free will.'' Whenever one's will crosses the will of God, the individual experiences discomfort, suffering, and disappointment.

The third type of suffering comes not as a result of previous actions but because there is an inherent value in the process of suffering. One learns a lesson that could not be gained otherwise and grows wiser as a result.

Religion holds that a person's biological life on Earth is an opportunity to live according to a code of moral and behavioral guidelines in such a way as to earn the privilege to enter into heaven after death and live with God. Heaven is the home of the divine creator and is a joyous place to abide.

If one does *not* do well according to the moral and behavioral codes, he will enter one of two other places, purgatory or hell (depending on which religious sect one belongs to). In purgatory the soul suffers hard for its sins, but as the name implies, it is eventually purged of its evil and freed to enter heaven. If, however, its sins are too grievous, the soul enters hell forever and it suffers excruciating pain without end.

Even though religion provides man with meaning and purpose, it leaves many important questions unanswered. Questions like: If this life is an opportunity to live in such a way as to earn the privilege to enter heaven, why then are we all not given the same opportunity to live this life well? Why are some souls born into environments of crime and sin while others are born into more constructive environments? Why are some of us born blind, crippled, diseased? Why are some of us robbed, raped, murdered, and so on? Why are some of us born into families where the tenets of the religion aren't accepted or even known? And, why does God create a soul who has no choice in the matter of his coming into being only to eternally punish him severely because he didn't live up to the code required?

Religion, as it has been taught in the West, allows for only one chance, one life, in order for us to prove worthy of entering heaven. The idea of having more than one life in which to learn and practice the moral and behavioral guidelines has had little, if any, place in mainstream Christianity. However, it was an accepted concept during the time of Christ, shortly after his resurrection and long before his birth. Furthermore, there is some evidence that the concepts of reincarnation were stricken from the church theology and even modified in the Bible at the Fifth Ecumenical Congress of Constantinople in A.D. 553. At this Congress, the works of the early church father, Origen, whose writings developed from the teachings of many earlier teachers, including Plato, were denounced and expunged from the Church's body of knowledge. Some references to reincarnation survived in other places, but most were lost forever.

Beyond the teachings and ideas of the church fathers, there are passages in the Bible, in Proverbs and Revelation and in the books of Matthew, Luke, and John, which may be further indication of an earlier acceptance of reincarnation. We'll get to some of these references later on.

## The Secret Teachings

There is another source for answers to the mysteries of life—what this book is all about, in fact. This source is not as organized and well-defined as science and religion, but its explanations hold together so well and are so comprehensive that they should be seriously considered.

Unfortunately, this source has no unifying name to its body of knowledge. Various parts of its principal concepts are actually scattered throughout different cultures and countries with no central collection point for the ideas. Because of this, and because many of its ideas are not widely known (often the adherents of these ideas have purposefully withheld them from the public in order to protect and preserve them), I'll refer to this school of thought as the "secret teachings." But it is not a single school of thought; rather, it's a hodgepodge of concepts from many diverse and often unrelated sources that reveal a very similar view of life and its meaning.

Science might categorize the secret teachings as *metaphysical*, meaning "beyond the known laws and observations of physics." Religion might refer to them as *mystical*, meaning that they belong to a collection of thought considered to be too mysterious to consider or of dubious origin.

It's interesting to note that the great religions have sects that know of and ascribe to some or all of the secret teachings. In Islam it would be the Sufis; in Judaism the Kabalists; in early Christianity, the Gnostics and later, from the Middle Ages through the Reformation to even modern times, the many Christian mystics.

Science, too, has had its adherents to concepts held by the secret teachings. Many scientists have written about theories of life beyond the physically observable. In some cases, phenomena have forced them to consider new theories.

As mentioned earlier, medicine has found that patients who have been declared dead, yet have been revived through the miracles of modern medicine, have reported witnessing the events occurring in the operating or emergency room while they were "dead." Since their bodies were obviously dead on the table, it should have been impossible for them to witness anything that transpired from the time they "died" until the time the doctors revived them. Though their stories vary, generally the patients claim to have been outside of their bodies, observing the whole process from above or across the room. They claim to have looked back and seen their bodies on the table. The doctors and nurses would then attempt to revive the body, using chemical stimulants, electricity, and physical manipulation, such as pounding on the heart. Later the doctor would come into the recovery room to see how his or her patient was doing only to hear a story that was impossible to explain according to current theories of life. These reports indicate that some part of an individual remains alive while the physical body is dead.

In another example, we find scientists observing that

learned traits may possibly be passed on to others without any means of physical contact. According to this story, which is referred to as the Hundredth Monkey, monkeys on one island learned to clean sand off their food by washing it in water. To the surprise of the scientists, monkeys on other islands, completely separated from the first monkeys, began washing their food in water before eating it. There seemed to be no way to explain this phenomenon other than the transmission of knowledge by some means beyond the usual physical, scientific norms of reality.

From such knowledge, some scientists are developing theories beyond physically observable phenomena, opening us up to a new vision of life—life beyond the physical.

But it is in the secret teachings that we are interested here, particularly those concerning reincarnation, for they possess many wonderful insights into the meaning of and purpose for our existence, giving us a much larger picture of life. In the following chapters they will be described in as much detail as I have been able to gather together from the many and varied sources I have studied over the years. In addition to mystical-religious and metaphysical-scientific sources, I've found elements of the secret teachings in obscure legends and myths, teachings of minor prophets and philosophers, and in the ancient records recovered by archaeologists. Much of my initial understanding of these teachings came from the work of the relatively modern (1877–1945) mystic and psychic, Edgar Cayce. In his material, some of which I'll review later in the book, I found my first introduction to these teachings. From there I discovered that many cultures possessed these ideas, though they were not always clearly defined or fully presented. I'll present the major elements of these teachings as cohesively as I can, along with a blend of my Western background and admitted perspective with some of the Eastern concepts.

Perhaps you'll find, as I have, that the secret teachings possess an unusually comprehensive view of life and answer many of the questions we've all considered to be unanswerable.

In order to understand life as it is seen in the secret teachings we must go back and retell the story of the original creation, for the well-known scientific and religious versions we've touched on are not quite correct.

# 2

## The Secret Genesis

IT'S DIFFICULT TO imagine the universe before the stars, the planets, the earth—before anything existed. But according to the secret teachings, prior to material creation, there was nothing, absolutely nothing . . . emptiness for as far as we could see and hear in any direction. Yet somewhere within this emptiness was the force, the "first impulse," that would begin the creation. We can think of this first consciousness as being similar to our own, except that it was boundless, a "Universal Consciousness." Before the beginning, the Universal Consciousness (and therefore the universe) was empty and still, without thought or image in its mind. But, it was alive and possessed the potential for thought, for creation. Using the image of our own consciousness, the creation would begin much like a clear mind begins to conceive an idea.

At some moment, this First Consciousness desired to express itself. Stirring from its silence, it began to conceive, to imagine and express its inner promptings. And so the creation began—light, sound . . . eventually stars, galaxies, trees, rivers, and so on. Remember, this is still prior to the physical creation that science records. It is a realm of thought. No physical forms exist. Perhaps if you close your eyes and imagine that only your thoughts and mental images exist, you can get a feel for it. The idea of light was conceived; the idea of a river, but not the physical form.

## A Part of the Whole

There came a point where the Creator's Consciousness desired to bring forth *companions*, creatures like itself that would share in this expression of life. They had to possess individual consciousness and freedom, so that they could choose to be companions. Otherwise, they would only have been servants of the Creator. So within the One Universal Consciousness many individual points of consciousness were awakened and given freedom.

It's important for us to realize that at this stage in our existence we did *not* have physical bodies. All of what I've just described occurred within the Mind of God. Consequently, our "form" resembled that of *thought* rather than physical object. In the very beginning we were individual points of consciousness within the one great Universal Consciousness.

We were still and quiet, our wills content to observe the wonders of the creation as they flowed from the Mind of God. In these early periods we were so much a part of the Creator's Consciousness that we were one with it, virtually indistinguishable from it. However, it wasn't long before some of us began to use our wills and express ourselves. At first, we simply imitated the Creator, but eventually we gained experience, and with experience came knowledge and confidence. Then, we truly began to create on our own, adding new dimensions to the whole, much like a second voice adds to a song by singing harmony with the main melody.

This is why we were created—to share in and contribute to the great expression of life and to be its companions. To fulfill this purpose we were made in the image of the Creator: consciousness with freedom; capable of conceiving, perceiving, and remembering; capable of communicating directly with the Creator and the other companions.

Consciousness and free will were the greatest qualities given any creation, but they came with equally great responsibility for their use or misuse. Of course, the all-knowing Universal One knew the potential dangers in giving beings complete freedom to do as they desired. However, the potential joy of sharing life with *true* companions, not servants, was deemed worth the risk. Therefore, each of these new free-willed beings would simply have to learn to take charge of themselves and to subdue harmful desires in order to live in harmony with the other companions and the Creator. To do otherwise would only bring chaos, suffering, and separation.

## The Fall of the Companions

Unfortunately, chaos came. As we continued to use our godly powers we became more fascinated with them. We began to focus more and more on our own creations and became less concerned with their harmony with the Creator. To experience our uniqueness and yet remain one with the whole was the ideal condition. But the more we thought of just ourselves and our own desires the more self-centered we became, eventually perceiving ourselves as separate from the whole.

Of course, this sense of separation was all in our heads, so to speak, because there really was no way we could exist outside of the whole. It was more a result of our sustained focus of attention on ourselves and our self-interests that resulted in a heightened sense of a distinct and separate self.

This was the beginning of trouble. It led to a very long fall that eventually left us feeling alone and separated from the rest of life. We, who were actually companions and cocreators with the Universal Creator, came to think of ourselves as little more than dustlike creatures, descendants of apes, and inhabitants of a planet on the outskirts of a typical galaxy in the endless and diverse universe.

The resulting loss of contact with the source of our life and the purpose for our existence was the beginning of darkness and evil. Without a clear sense of our relationship to the rest of life, many of us began to use free will in ways that were never meant to be. Others simply let themselves be carried along with the current of life, abdicating their free will to others. In both cases, our naive curiosity, combined with a reckless disregard for the consequences of our actions and thoughts and our relentless self-seeking, caused us to do and experience many things that we would come to regret—things that would make it very difficult for us to be companions to the Creator.

However, the Creator foresaw this potential and, prior to creating companions, it created a Universal Law: Whatever one did with its free will, it must experience. The law was not intended as punishment or retribution for offenses, but as a tool for education and enlightenment. Thus, as we used our freedom we experienced the effects. In this way we came to understand and learn.

Interestingly, science and religion recognize this law. In science it is often stated, "For every action there is a reaction." Its religious counterpart is, "An eye for an eye, a tooth for a tooth"; "As you sow, so shall you reap"; and "As you do unto others, it will be done unto you." Even the kids on our streets know something of this law, expressing its principle in their saying, "What goes around, comes around."

This is the law of karma, of cause and effect. It is the great teacher of the companions-to-be, and it is an integral part of the secret teachings. However, as we will see in a later chapter, the secret teachings develop an entire vision of life around the tireless, precise workings of this fundamental law of the universe.

## Spirit, Mind, and Soul

Once the law was established, the Creator awakened countless independent points of consciousness and the companions came into being. What a trembling wonder it must have been in those first moments.

Again, it's important to realize that the companions were not physical bodies. They were like "ideas" in the mind of the Creator that were given freedom to be independently conscious. As they used their freedom they evolved into unique points of thought, feeling, desire, expression, and memory. *They* began developing ideas, becoming clearer and more uniquely defined and identifiable as they experienced life. But like an idea, their true "form" was consciousness.

In order to further understand the companions' nature, I'll describe their makeup using terms we are familiar with today. Each has spirit, mind, and soul.

Spirit is the essence of life. Remember the condition of the Creator *before* the creation; alive yet still. Nothing existed, but life was latent in the emptiness like a consciousness without a thought. This is spirit, as I'm defining it here. It is the living stillness in the midst of activity. So often we identify life with motion, but the essence of life, spirit, was there before the motion.

Life in motion, or the power to move and shape ideas and even physical forms out of spirit, is mind. Mind is the sculptor, the builder who conceives, imagines, and shapes ideas out of the essence of life. Spirit is life; mind is the power to use it.

Using these definitions, and contrary to what science tells us, a rock would be considered alive. Spirit's presence in the rock is certainly different from its presence in the amoeba, but a rock has spirit. Mind has shaped this aspect of life into a hard, seemingly motionless form, but, as the Native Americans always knew, rock has spirit.

Each of the companions had spirit and mind. As they used their life forces they developed experiences, memories, desires, fears, etc. This caused them to become unique from one another—each having its own collection of experiences and aspirations; each its own story. This individual aspect of the companion is its soul. Soul is the sum total of all the companion has done with its free-willed consciousness. It's the companion's story, its complex of memories. All of the companions have spirit and mind but each developed a unique soul, because each built a different collection of memories and experiences, resulting in different desires, hopes, and attitudes about life.

As you can see, the soul developed, grew, and changed, just as it continues to do in the present. It changes as the individual experiences life and gradually builds its own collection of memories that result in a unique character.

Spirit is the life force, mind is the power to use it, and soul is the being that develops. All are one in consciousness.

## Into the Earth

The creation progressed from essence to thought, from thought into thought form, and from thought form into particle form or atomic form—in other words, matter. There are many dimensions to life. One of them is the third dimension, which is physical form as we know it today.

The companions, filled with their new-found consciousness and freedom, went out into the vast universe to experience life and to learn about themselves, the Creator, and their relationship to it. In their travels through the cosmos, some of the companions decided to investigate the three-dimensional influences of the planet Earth, where they entered into physical form for the first time. Here they became so encapsulated in the physical that they began to identify themselves more with their form than with their consciousness. They began to think of themselves as physical entities rather than living consciousnesses. To have an individual body was the ultimate in self-identity, self-expression. But incredibly, these celestial beings began to think they were only terrestrial beings. Their physical form was so substantial, so captivating, that it was difficult to hold on to the more delicate reality of spirit-thoughts.

Strong identification with the physical made the companions subject to the laws of nature, and, of course, a part of nature's cycle was death. The body would come to life according to the laws of nature, live for a time, and then die. In their original state, the companions were continually alive, but those that began to strongly identify with their physical bodies were now affected by death. Since they thought they *were* their bodies, they considered themselves dead when their bodies died. And, for all intents and purposes, they *were* dead. "As the mind thinketh, so it is."

This was a serious confusion, and when the companions who had not become involved with the Earth saw what had happened, they decided to help those on Earth regain their former state. However, it was not going to be easy. The earthbound companions had continued in this masquerade for so long that they were deeply possessed by the belief that the physical world was the *real* world, even to the point that all else seemed like phantoms and dreams. Life for them had become totally physical. They considered themselves lucky to live a long physical life, expecting to eventually die like all those that had come before them. That's as far as their limited vision could take them.

In addition to the influences of the physical dimension, the souls were building reaction patterns (karmic patterns) with their willful activities in the physical world. According to the universal law, these actions had to be met—properly met in the physical where they had been initiated. So the web was becoming more and more entangled and complex. The more one acted in the Earth environs, the more one built Earth debts that had to be met in future Earth reactions. There were going to be no quick outs for anyone. Once a soul touched the physical, it was certain to become obsessed and confused by the very nature of the realm. The only joys found in the physical would be those of the spirit, and those would be so delicate or intangible that holding on to them would be difficult—not impossible, but difficult.

Of course, the pleasures of the physical would be fulfilling to the physical aspect of these incarnated souls, but it would not sustain them for very long. They were children of the cosmos, celestial beings; terrestrial pleasures could only hold their interests for so long before they desired experiences more true to their real nature. Yet, by the very nature of the flesh, it would be hard to free the spirit from it.

## A House Divided

Another effect of entering the Earth plane was the division of consciousness. According to the concepts found in the Edgar Cayce revelations (see Appendix 1 for background on Edgar Cayce), as an individual entered deeper into the physical, its consciousness separated into three divisions of awareness. Two of these divisions we acknowledge today, the conscious and subconscious.

The first entails the physical world where the human body required a three-dimensional consciousness to function in the Earth. It has become the part of our consciousness we are most familiar with, what we have come to call the *conscious* mind. Many of us would consider it to actually be the "I" or "me" of ourselves. It is within this part of consciousness that we experience physical life and our personalities are developed. In many ways it is our Earth-self.

The second part of consciousness is shadowlike while one is incarnate. It lives life like a shadow, always there, listening, watching, remembering, and only occasionally making its profound and sometimes frightening presence known. We have come to call this part of our consciousness the *subconscious* mind. From out of this area come dreams, intuitions, unseen motivations, and deepest memories.

Often the thoughts and interests of the conscious mind, combined with the desires of the body, become so strong and dominant that only its activities seem important and real; the subconscious seems illusionary and unrelated to outer life. But in truth, the real life is occurring in the subconscious. We'll explore this later on.

The third area of the now divided consciousness is the most universal. It is the part that can perceive and commune with the Universal Consciousness. We have different names for it: the Collective Mind, the Universal Mind, the Collective Unconscious, and Cayce's term, the *Superconscious*.

As the diagram illustrates, the more one's attention moves into the conscious mind, the more narrow and limited the focus and awareness become. This is where we see ourselves as being only physical and we lose touch with the Creator. The more one moves toward the superconscious, the more one becomes aware of the whole, the Universal Forces, the Creator.

## The Paradox

It may be more difficult to perceive the infinite when one is grossly involved in physical life, but the Universal Consciousness and the potential for attuning oneself to it remain. Curiously, the way to make contact is through the inner consciousness of the incarnate individual and not outside of it, making it a very mysterious passage for a physical being. In other words, the companions went out to explore the universe with the equipment to "phone home" already in place within their consciousness.

The Creator knew that in time the earthbound companions could again become aware of the difference between terrestrial life and celestial. They could again come to know their original state and purpose and regain their celestial birthright of companionship with the Creator. In time they could again come to realize that the conditions in their present physical life were the result of their free-will actions and choices *before* the present life.

They could even come again to know themselves as cocreators with *the* Creator. (The Creator is considered to

The Universal Consciousness

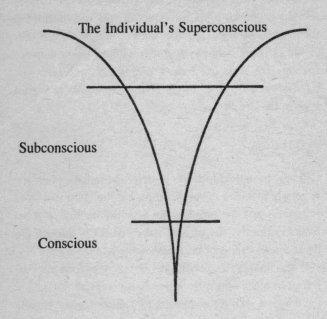

The Individual's Superconscious

Subconscious

Conscious

The Collective Unconscious
communicating telepathically

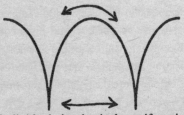

Individuals in physical manifestation
communicating with the 5 senses

be nonsexed, complete unto itself, but our language does not allow for a pronoun to express this nature, so I'll occasionally use "he/she" or "him/her" to keep from masculinizing the Creator. I'll also use the neutral pronoun, "it," to keep from personifying the Universal Consciousness too much. It is personal, but not a person as we know them.)

If the earthbound souls could genuinely believe that the physical cannot possibly be all there is to life, they could begin the long journey back from form to spirit, a very difficult journey. One simply cannot think of oneself as a lump of flesh, blood, and bone one minute and as ethereal, spirit form in the next minute. The influences of finite form on an infinite being are profoundly stupefying. In many ways we, as human beings, are no longer spirit. Flesh has become very much a part of us, not just physically but mentally as well. Even when we are out of the body (through death, deep sleep, or some altered state), bodily manifestation is still very much a part of us. Otherwise, there would certainly be no reincarnation. We would simply leave and never return.

The great paradox of man is that he is now both spirit and flesh. That's like saying we are a combination of oil and water, two substances that do not combine. I suppose the mystical analogy would more properly be fire and water. How can anything be made up of two substances that are impossible to combine? Yet, such is the nature of humanity. We are constantly forced to reconcile the seemingly irreconcilable: mercy with justice, cooperation with independence, unity with diversity, tradition with change, feeling with thought, love with truth, and on and on. In the Cayce material, the warning to seekers of enlightenment is often, *seek a balance!* Perhaps this is also the intention behind Jesus' teaching that, "in patience possess ye your soul." Patience is certainly required if one is to reconcile spirit with flesh.

# 3

# A Stellar Dimension

ENTERING THE INFLUENCES of the Earth was not a quick, single transition from spirit to form, from universal to physical consciousness, but a long descent through many levels of consciousness and realms of activity. It also didn't begin with the Earth. Souls experienced many parts of the universe, including other planets. Many still do. Even more fascinating is the concept that soul is not bound to the physical world even when incarnate! Depending on its level of awareness, a soul may experience other dimensions during physical life.

According to the secret teachings, and particularly the Edgar Cayce material, Earth is not the only planet that attracts souls. As strange as it may sound given our current scientific beliefs, souls descending from out of the great cosmos actually entered into this *entire* solar system, not just the Earth. They have had and continue to have experiences with other planets in this system, and some of the moons, and even the sun! Now, let me explain this before all my credibility vanishes.

## Among the Stars and Planets

The souls, being nonphysical, were and are capable of sojourning in realms of consciousness beyond the third dimension, which is physical. This doesn't mean they live *on the surface* of other planets as we do on Earth, but rather in fourth- and fifth-dimensional realms *associated* with the planetary spheres. The physical planets are also *nonphysical realms* that souls can experience when not actively in the physical body on Earth. This would include death, deep sleep, or other altered states that free the subconscious from its normal physical constraints.

Furthermore, each of the planets is a unique environ with activities that differ from other planets in this system. These activities can effect various changes in souls that experience them. It's as if the solar system were a university in which the planets were various colleges within the university—a great big schoolhouse for the souls.

If a soul incarnates into an Earth life from one of the planetary influences, it will manifest the influence of the realm from which it recently came. This is why astrology has so interested man since early history. The stars and planets have influence on people's lives. Unfortunately, most of our modern astrologers have lost the original knowledge of why they do. It is, according to the secret teachings, because reincarnating souls have not been in limbo prior to their return to Earth but have actually been "traveling" among the stars and planets. (Remember, I am not talking about the physical stars and planets but dimensions associated with the physical objects we see.) At the moment of birth, the position of the heavens gives some idea as to

where the incarnating soul has been, and this in turn gives
some idea of how he or she will behave in the current
incarnation.

## Planetary Influences

Let's look at each of these planets and their unique characteristics. They are very similar to what astrology teaches
us. What follows are Edgar Cayce's descriptions of each
planet's major influence on a soul:

*Mercury* pertains to the mind and the mental abilities.

*Venus* pertains to love, beauty, and the arts.

*Earth* pertains to the flesh and the ability to actually prove
one's inner beliefs through outer actions.

*Mars* pertains to "madness" (Cayce's word), or the power
of force, temper, and drive—unless tempered by the mental forces.

*Jupiter* pertains to strength, universality, expansiveness—
dealing with groups or masses rather than individuals.

*Saturn* pertains always to change—usually sudden or violent change; a preference to erase all and start over again.
It is where flesh goes to purge itself (more on this in the
chapter on Leila).

*Uranus* pertains to the psychic abilities and occult
sciences—and to extremes, such as: great goodness or
badness, great wealth or poverty, etc.

*Neptune* pertains to the mystic abilities, spiritual insight,
and a sense of the unseen—also some extremes unless
tempered.

*Pluto* (possibly the same as Septimus and Vulcan) pertains

to consciousness, usually spiritual consciousness. Cayce said the influence of this planet is just beginning to enter Earth's environs.

The Cayce material indicates that an individual incarnating from the far-away planets of Uranus, Neptune, and Pluto will seem peculiar and will have difficulty being understood, while those incarnating from the nearby planets will seem more natural. Those from Venus will be inclined toward interests of love, caring, beauty, and the arts. Those incarnating from Mercury will have a more intellectual, logical, mental approach to life, as opposed to the Venusians' feelings, emotions, and cares of the heart. A soul who incarnates directly from a sojourn in the influences of Mars will possess urges to seek his or her way with force and power, influenced by temper and drive (unless such urges have been subdued; in this case, the soul may become a dynamic "doer" who also has patience). General Patton, a believer in reincarnation, felt he was a son of Mars, a natural warrior. When we consider the "stellar dimension," he was probably correct. We could assume, following this concept, that his soul incarnated directly from a sojourn in the realms of Mars, bringing with it all the qualities that Mars would bestow on a soul.

Of course, many of us have experienced several planets from which we reflect multiple influences. Often Cayce would identify three or four planets as contributing to a person's total makeup. The "aspects" of planets one to another help to reveal a more complete picture of an individual's planetary influences. Multiple experiences also help to build a more balanced, multidimensional soul.

Judging from Patton's strengths, Mars would certainly have been a dominant force in his soul's experiences. But his weaknesses reveal limitations in the areas of diplomacy, compromise, and patience. Perhaps a few sojourns in Jupiter would have added helpful aspects to his character. And, according to the Cayce readings, this is exactly what may have occurred after his death. His soul, reflecting on the recent incarnation, may have decided that some new experiences were in order and began a sojourn in the fourth dimensional realms of some "college" other than Mars.

Let's look at another example. According to the Cayce readings, the soul that came to be known as Edgar Cayce sojourned in the realms of Uranus prior to its incarnation as Edgar Cayce. On its way to Earth it briefly visited the environs of Venus. These two influences were in part responsible for Cayce's *innate* tendencies toward things of the psychic and an appreciation of beauty and art and the power of love.

Planetary influences of the type I've described here, as opposed to astrology as it is practiced today, manifest themselves almost immediately in a child's preferences and approach to life. When the karmic influences (from previous *Earth* sojourns, not planetary sojourns) begin to manifest themselves (this usually occurs at or near puberty), then the combination of the planetary influences and the Earthly karmic influences makes for the rocky teenage years.

# 4

## The Physical Body

WHEN THE COMPANIONS began to enter Earth life, only the plant, animal, and mineral kingdoms existed here. Many of the first to arrive took over whatever physical forms were available and just pushed their way into three-dimensional life. The bizarre creatures that remain in our legends today were the result of this forceful entry into early Earth: *satyrs* (beings that were half goat and half man), *centaurs* (half horse and half man), *dryads* (women living in trees, and often an entire "enchanted" forest of them), *sphinxes* (half man and half lion, ram, or hawk; also a winged lion with a woman's head and breasts), and *mermaids* (half woman and half fish).

## The Evolutionary Chain

Souls that did not immediately force their way in could see that assuming possession of these lower forms was not good; they desired to perfect a form specifically for the companions. In this way the companions could manifest in a body more reflective of who they really were and not defy the law of nature, which stated that all creatures should give life only to their own kind.

The rescuing souls began influencing the evolutionary cycles of the Earth forms until they could breed a form that closely approximated their ideal. The form they chose was indeed that of the apes, as our scientists have so carefully observed. Hovering over these ape creatures like Olympian gods, the companions used their creative powers to alter the monkey forms—something like a breeder would do to create a new species.

The next step required the help of the Creator. In order for the form to be perfect for the companions, it needed to be enlivened by the original Creator of life. The companions had the power to create, but the final form for manifesting in the Earth needed that special spark of life that only the Creator could give. The Creator knew the needs of its lost companions and their hearts and lovingly added the final touch to the human body. Perhaps this is why there remains a "missing link" in the evolutionary chain, for the creative leap from ape to man is physically untraceable.

Once the human body was perfected, all those with strange, mixed-up bodies were corrected, until the companions were inhabiting only human bodies. No more human souls would incarnate in animal, plant, or mineral forms. The concept of transmigration is a carryover from this early period, but it no longer occurs. In fact, the level of power possessed by most incarnating souls today is barely sufficient for them to completely possess human bodies.

## The Realm of Duality

The perfected bodies were then separated into two sexual forms, a male and a female. The companions had been androgynous in their spirit "form," male and female in one, but in order for them to manifest in the realm of duality of flesh and spirit, it was necessary to divide the two sexual aspects of soul.

Therefore, only one sexual aspect of an incarnate soul became dominantly manifested; usually it reflected the sex of the physical body, but not always. A soul could be manifesting its female aspect and yet incarnate in a male body. In such a case, we would see an effeminate male; in the reverse, we would see a masculine female. Usually, however, the male sexual aspect of the soul is expressed through a male body during incarnation, and the female aspect in a female body.

There were many reasons for separating these two sexual aspects of the soul while incarnating, the chief one being, of all things, loneliness. Togetherness in the celestial realm was natural, but the third dimension required clear demarcations of space and time. The souls were alone inside spacially separated bodies, and not only was it more difficult to companion with fellow souls, but because of the loss of contact with the Creator, they felt completely on their own. Therefore it was deemed best to separate the female and male aspects and create a relationship where two souls could reunite on the Earth and give some sense of wholeness and togetherness to earthly life. It also provided a physically natural way to reproduce themselves according to the laws of nature. This would become very important as

the companions continued to lose more and more cogni-
zance of their spiritual selves, eventually becoming totally
physical—completely subject to the laws of nature and without the supernatural powers they had possessed prior to this
time.

## Spiritual Centers

The body that was eventually developed for the companions is like our body today. It possesses physical, mental,
and spiritual aspects. These parts are so closely blended
together that the impressions of one have an effect on the
other two: what one eats can affect one's thinking; thinking
can affect digestion; spiritual inspiration can affect physical
conditions; and so on. This is the vehicle of God's companions while they abide in the material plane and, as such,
it has become the temple of the "living God."

According to nearly all the secret teachings, within this
body are seven spiritual centers through which the soul
manifests in the three-dimensional world. These centers (or
*chakras*, as they are known in Eastern teachings) are associated with the endocrine glands and certain plexuses along
the cerebrospinal and sympathetic nervous systems.
Through these channels the forces of the spiritual reach into
three-dimensional form, providing the means for the incarnate soul to reattune to its spiritual self and the Universal
Consciousness.

These seven centers correlate with the seven colors of the
spectrum that appear when a beam of white light is re-
fracted. The symbology is subtly beautiful: the central,
whole being is like a beam of white light; as it passes

through physical dimensions, represented by the prism (symbolizing the body), only its parts are seen.

The centers also correlate with the seven notes of the musical scale and to seven major planets in our solar system, as indicated in the diagram and chart. The four lower centers correlate with the four elements of the Earth plane: earth, wind, water, and fire. The four lower centers symbolize the Earth, while the three higher centers reflect Heaven.

The body of the companions is a reflection of their cosmic, universal selves, and as such, it is a temporary, terrestrial home for celestial beings.

## Original Sin

From the secret teachings we now know that the two sexual aspects of the soul were separated into man and woman and that their physical bodies served as the vehicles for God's companions. We also know that they were actually celestial beings who became terrestrial by their own doing and eventually thought of themselves as little more than bodies. Furthermore, being in the physical plane was *not* their ultimate purpose for existence. It was hoped they would come to know and love God enough to seek his/her companionship *in the spirit*, not in the flesh (John 4:23–24). With all of this in mind, let's review the Genesis story of original sin.

The earthbound souls, now represented by Adam and Eve, were forbidden to eat the fruit from the "Tree of the Knowledge of Good and Evil." If they did, as the serpent well knew (Gen. 3:4–5), they would realize that they were

## SPIRITUAL CENTERS OF THE BODY

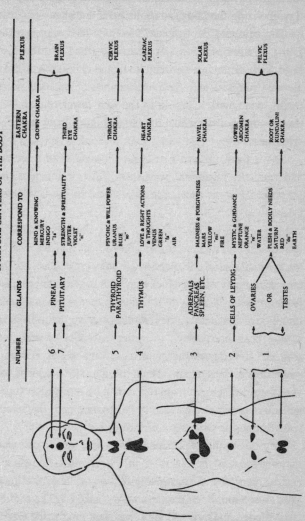

| NUMBER | GLANDS | CORRESPOND TO | EASTERN CHAKRA | PLEXUS |
|---|---|---|---|---|
| 6 | PINEAL | MIND & KNOWING MERCURY INDIGO "la" | CROWN CHAKRA | BRAIN PLEXUS |
| 7 | PITUITARY | STRENGTH & SPIRITUALITY JUPITER VIOLET "si" | THIRD EYE CHAKRA | |
| 5 | THYROID PARATHYROID | PSYCHIC & WILL POWER URANUS BLUE "so" | THROAT CHAKRA | CERVIC PLEXUS |
| 4 | THYMUS | LOVE & RIGHT ACTIONS & THOUGHTS VENUS GREEN "fa" AIR | HEART CHAKRA | CARDIAC PLEXUS |
| 3 | ADRENALS PANCREAS SPLEEN, ETC. | MADNESS & FORGIVENESS MARS YELLOW "mi" FIRE | NAVEL CHAKRA | SOLAR PLEXUS |
| 2 | CELLS OF LEYDIG | MYSTIC & GUIDANCE NEPTUNE ORANGE "re" WATER | LOWER ABDOMEN CHAKRA | PELVIC PLEXUS |
| 1 | OVARIES OR TESTES | FLESH & BODILY NEEDS SATURN RED "do" EARTH | ROOT OR KUNDALINI CHAKRA | |

really gods within God and had free will to do whatever
they pleased. (The serpent neglected to tell them that they
had already used their free will to force their way into the
Earth, an act they would not have been proud of if they had
known the difference between good and evil.) And, if they
ate the fruit and learned the difference before they were
ready, their shame and guilt would so overwhelm them that
they would not want to be near God's all-knowing consciousness. Thus, restricting their awareness of good and
evil gave them time to live in God's *manifested* presence
and gradually regain an awareness of their true nature and
purpose, all in the protection represented by the Garden of
Eden.

Metaphysically, the ''garden'' is the illusion created by
time and space, two phenomena that do not actually exist in
the spiritual realm. Time and space were created to give the
companions a reality in which they could change or progress
from one state of being to a higher state by correcting and
improving. Eventually, they would perceive themselves as
having been born anew, or, using a biblical description
from the Revelation, they would perceive their soiled gar-
ments to be clean again. Their transgressions against the
very source that gave them life would be resolved in time,
and space gave them a place to be separate until they were
ready to be one with the All-Knowing.

But once again the companions-to-be chose to do what
they wanted, and they ate the fruit! The resulting knowledge
caused them to feel immense guilt, so much so that they
''hid from God,'' feeling they were ''naked.'' The awareness of good and evil and the subsequent guilt made God's
efforts to help them even more difficult. Now they were

going to have to go even farther away from God's presence until they could feel redeemed enough to seek and abide in his/her presence again (Rev. 7:14).

The author of Genesis subtly reveals this growing distance from God by changing his name as the companions continue to move farther away. Accordingly, man was first created by "God," but when he entered the physical world his body was made by the "Lord God," with whom he shared the garden. Finally, after the loss of the garden, he related to the divine as "Lord."

For a long time things got progressively worse. Cain and Abel could only relate to their Creator through altar sacrifices. Eventually, the people could not even conduct their own altar sacrifices; it had to be done for them by an anointed one—a priest, prophet, or holy man. Still later they wanted one of their members to be appointed king over them so he could tell them what to do (I Samuel, chap. 8). Their personal, direct relationship with the Creator was becoming blocked by layers of protective barriers, until the people no longer knew they were each meant to be direct, personal companions to the Creator. In fact, this was the principal crime that led to Jesus' being sentenced to death: he claimed to be the "Son of God," in personal touch with God, and God was his *father*! This claim was too much for the authorities to accept; no man was that closely related to God. This shows just how far away from their true nature man had come.

Let's return to the garden again. Since the souls had come to know what they had done and who they were by eating the forbidden fruit, it was imperative that their hiding from the Creator not go on forever. After all, they were supposed to become the companions of the Creator. And so, the fruit from the Tree of Life (representing unlimited access to the spirit, and therefore, immortality) was taken away from them and protected from them. They would no longer have unlimited access to life's "power source" as they had before this fall. Now they would have only as much life or spirit as they *sought* through attunement to the spirit while incarnate. The less they remained attuned to their true life source, the more they had to consume what little of the élan vital (life/spirit force) they had. When it ran out, they could no longer sustain their bodies and they died, leaving them without physical vehicles in which to manifest. In this way they were unable to make a permanent home in the third dimension as terrestrial beings, and they were forced to experience and refamiliarize themselves with the other dimensions from which they had originally come.

# 5

## To The Rescue!

THE SOULS WHO remained near the Earth but outside its influence were in a position to help the earthbound souls. At first they entered straight into the physical to help reawaken the others, but when they found themselves distracted, confused, and captivated by their form, they wisely decided to regroup and reconsider more carefully how they might achieve a rescue. It quickly became apparent that the physical dimension was a far more difficult problem than anyone had at first imagined. No matter how good one's intentions, once the transition from soul-in-consciousness to soul-in-substance was made, it was nearly impossible to retain an awareness of one's true nature. Substance was too consuming, and one couldn't just touch it and then leave it. To use an old Southern concept, it was like grabbing hold of a tar baby—once you touched it, it had a hold of you.

### Behind the Mask

In some ways, entering physical form can be compared to attending a costume ball. In order to get in you have to put on a costume, and once in costume you and those around you begin to think of each other as being the image of the costumes. After playing this game long enough, you become so familiar with the costume reality that it becomes the dominant reality. You forget everyone is really a person in a costume. And, of course, to add to the confusion, the ball is very exciting, filled with lights, music, foods of all kinds, dancing, and activities galore! Your entire focus becomes the ball, the costumes, the adventure; the party seems to go on forever. But the longer you stay, the more your costume wears away, until it is worn thin, and you can't use it any longer. Without a costume you must leave. If you want to return, you must find another costume. Then, you enter the party again. Before you know it, everything revolves around the ball and your efforts to stay at the ball—or return to it with a new costume. Everyone has by now forgotten that within the bodies are real souls, and beyond the physical world is an entire spiritual universe with a Creator who wants to share it.

Helping the souls at the "costume ball" was going to be a real challenge. They were now so focused on the ball and the costumes that they could only be communicated with *at the ball* and *in costume*. The rescuing souls were going to have to risk getting themselves lost in the cycle of life and death in order to communicate with the others. Ultimately, all the souls that touched the physical would have to experience the separation of consciousness and the blinding limitations of three-dimensional reality—and then somehow overcome it! There was simply no easy way in and out; one had to come to terms with it until no longer possessed by it.

To protect against the complete loss of the truth, the

rescuing souls wove the real story about the companions and their predicament into the fabric of physical life, into its legends and myths, its art and symbols. Thus, when any lost soul looked beyond what he found in physical life, the truth would be there for him or her to rediscover.

## Fairy Tales, Legends, and Myths

We don't have to go very far to find references to the companions and their dilemma. The story is told again and again in many of the classic fairy tales we learned as children. Some examples of the stories that hold the treasures of the ancient truth are *Sleeping Beauty*, *Snow White*, and *Pinocchio*. Each of these compelling tales has a theme based on the battle between good and evil for possession of an innocent person who wants only to live happily ever after. Despite all efforts to prevent it, the innocent one is killed by evil, but eventually comes to life again through the forces of good and experiences the full measure of his or her dreams.

In Sleeping Beauty's tale, her marriage to the prince is doomed when she pricks her finger on a spinning wheel and dies, but the penalty is reduced from eternal death to "a deep sleep." Through the prince's efforts to free himself from the grips of evil and to defeat the dragon, he is able to reach Sleeping Beauty and awaken her.

Snow White's marriage to a prince is also doomed because she eats the apple that evil presents to her and dies, but she is not really dead, only in a deep sleep. After searching long and hard, the prince finally finds her in the forest and awakens her with a kiss.

In Pinocchio's tale we find a wooden boy who can become a real boy only if he proves himself worthy. In his efforts to live the way he should, Pinocchio falls prey to many of evil's distractions; each has a devastating effect on him, and the last challenge kills him. But because he was trying to save Geppetto in those final minutes of life, Pinocchio is granted the promise of the good fairy and comes alive again as a real boy.

In the tales of Sleeping Beauty and Snow White, the soul of a companion is symbolized by the beautiful, innocent princess. The prince symbolizes the mind of the companion. He is the companion's power to reason, understand, and perceive so that he can cut through the illusionary powers and darkness of evil and reunite with his soul. It is the light of understanding that shines through the darkness and reveals the truth. In these two tales the mind had to struggle with many powerful illusions before it could possess its soul.

Sleeping Beauty's loss of consciousness by pricking her finger on her spinning wheel is symbolic of the soul's entry into flesh and blood through the use of its free will (spinning its pattern). The evil fairy who predicts the coming doom and eventually grows into the fiery dragon who challenges the mind's efforts to revive the soul is the evil of self—self-glorification, self-aggrandizement, self-centeredness, and self-willfulness—all to the detriment of the soul.

We encounter this same evil power personified in the stepmother-queen of Snow White. "Mirror, mirror on the wall, who's the fairest of them all?" As we will see later in the legend of the Fallen Angels, this self-centered vanity is a major stumbling block to spiritual consciousness and true freedom.

In *Pinocchio* we have an even clearer picture of the companion's struggle. Pinocchio (the individual soul) cannot become a real companion and share the full meaning of companionship with his father (the heavenly father), who created him, until *he comes to terms with his freedom to choose*. Of course, his conscience shows him the way. Here, as well as in true life, concern for others is a major step in recovering from the self-centered use of free will. Pinocchio's selfless concern for Geppetto resurrected him from death and transformed him into the boy he was always meant to be.

Another tale that contains elements of the story of the companions is *The Wizard of Oz*. In this one the soul, as Dorothy, finds herself in a strange land far from home. In her quest to get back to Kansas she meets three aspects of herself that are lacking something: heart (the tin man), mind (the scarecrow), and courage or will (the lion). By following the path replete with trials, she arrives at the wizard's castle only to find that the way home was within her all the time. So it is with the companions of God who are in the Earth. Of course, before we return, we have to take away the broom from the last remaining wicked witch, freeing the land of her tyranny!

Perhaps the ultimate example of the companions' separation from the Creator is found in the well-known story of the Fallen Angels. Here we find the basic theme again but with a curious twist.

In heaven there was an angel of such beauty and brilliance that he was called "the Morning Star." His name was Lucifer. Lucifer began to think that he was the most beautiful being in the heavens. He was so beautiful that he felt others should consider his nature and defer to it. He began to do as he pleased and encouraged others to follow him. His thoughts of the Universal, nonpersonified Creator that made him were lost, and he was pulling others away with him.

Once the rebellion was discovered, God brought forth his archangel, Michael, to throw Lucifer and his followers out of Heaven to protect it from any further rebellion. Michael cast them into Hell and Earth where they ruled until a Redeemer was sent to resurrect them to their former state.

A penance was decided upon by God and the other angels. Lucifer must subordinate his will to the will of God until he preferred God's will to his own. In addition, he must help those angels he encouraged to rebel by showing them his preference for God's will over his own. If this were done, the Morning Star would shine again in the heavens.

In this legend we have the whole story of the companions' struggle with free will and independent consciousness, though it is difficult to consider the lost companions as being symbolized by Lucifer and his fellow angels! But according to the secret teachings, *they* are the fallen angels, lost to their original purpose and nature through their own self-glorifying use of free will. But, even Lucifer was given life by God, and because God wishes that not one of his creations be lost forever, a way was prepared for all to return to their former place.

## The Passage Through The Realm

And so the pattern for a soul's involvement in the Earth was set. It would sojourn in the third dimension in a human body and live in time and space, physical form and duality.

The realm would be "the Land of Choice." Here each soul would have opportunities to choose between the fulfillment of self and the fulfillment of one's purpose with the Divine. It was hoped that the soul would apply itself to the positive choices that were presented in this unique place. By selecting good over evil, truth over falsehood, others' needs over one's wants, the harmony of the whole over the pleasures of selfishness, the companion would then reach beyond self and seek again a conscious awareness of the Creator. All of this would require learning to use free will properly and getting control over the forces and illusions of the physical world. Furthermore, the soul would have to meet the consequences of its own actions—healing the wounds it had inflicted on itself and others, righting the wrongs, and untying the fetters it had placed on itself and others.

By making the right choices and living more and more like a companion of the Creator, the soul could regain its previous consciousness and state. But it was a tremendously difficult task, requiring a very long time, by Earth standards. Many cycles of being in the body and in the spirit were needed.

With each physical life came a whole new set of opportunities. The soul's task was not only to desire the former state of spirit consciousness and companionship with the Creator, but actually to *live it* through actions and thoughts. By choosing the eternal over the temporary, harmony over discord, cooperation over rebellion, and the Universal over self, the soul would come to know its true nature. The more one chose the fruits of the spirit, the more one became the spirit again, freeing oneself of the possessive powers of the physical. Eventually, this would lead to a new awareness of actually being a soul *manifesting* a body rather than just a body.

With each death in the physical came the birth again into the spirit and the opportunity to reflect on how well the individual used its most recent incarnation. The memories and impressions left from the soul's incarnation gave it strength and encouragement for completing the task of the reunion. As one proved to itself that it not only desired the former state but actually lived it and chose it, one gained strength over its guilt and doubt, and came again into the presence of the all-knowing God, its Father/Mother and Companion.

Now that the passage through the difficult physical dimension and back to the Creator was established, there remained only for some soul to go through it and reach the other side. By doing so, the way would be clearer and easier for others to get through. But who would go first? Most of the lost ones were so busy with their own pursuits that they didn't even care about the passage. Many others longed to return home and regain their true place, yet they were doubtful, weak, and weary of the effort required. According to some of the secret teachings and those of Edgar Cayce, the first soul to volunteer to go through every trial, overcome every temptation, dispel every illusion, conquer every challenge, and reach perfection was that soul we call Jesus of Nazareth.

## The First Begotten Son

> "No man has ascended up
> to heaven but he that came
> down from heaven, even the
> Son of man. . . ."
>
> JESUS CHRIST (John 3:13)

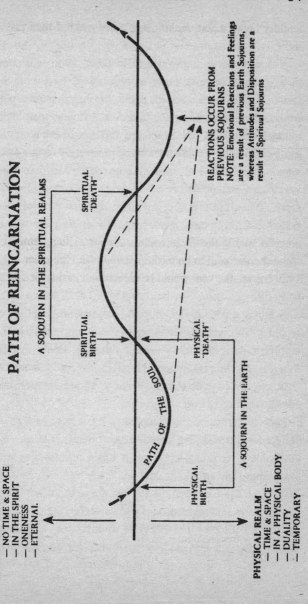

# PATH OF REINCARNATION

A SOJOURN IN THE SPIRITUAL REALMS

SPIRITUAL "DEATH"

SPIRITUAL BIRTH

PHYSICAL "DEATH"

PATH OF THE SOUL

PHYSICAL BIRTH

A SOJOURN IN THE EARTH

REACTIONS OCCUR FROM PREVIOUS SOJOURNS
NOTE: Emotional Reactions and Feelings are a result of previous Earth Sojourns, whereas Attitudes and Disposition are a result of Spiritual Sojourns

SPIRITUAL REALM
— NO TIME & SPACE
— IN THE SPIRIT
— ONENESS
— ETERNAL

PHYSICAL REALM
— TIME & SPACE
— IN A PHYSICAL BODY
— DUALITY
— TEMPORARY

This soul entered the world of form and "dwelt among us," living through every phase of physical life. He did not accomplish this in one physical lifetime, as we are commonly led to believe, nor was he born perfect, as some insist. He was born a human being, but he assumed a purpose and mission that made him very different from most humans. He lived like a normal person, experienced the same temptations, weaknesses, and distractions that all humans experience. But, through compliance with the Universal Law and the Father's Will, he overcame the physical world. Thus did this soul regain its former state of consciousness, fulfilling its great purpose—showing the way to all who would choose to follow. By doing this, Jesus became the model, the way, the example (in Cayce's words, "the ensample") for all souls in and around the influences of Earth.

Not only did he do this in Earth, but according to Cayce, he did it with each planetary realm in this system! Thus, he perfected mind (Mercury), heart (Venus), flesh (Earth), "madness" (Mars), strength (Jupiter), the force of change (Saturn), the psychic (Uranus), the mystic (Neptune), and consciousness (Pluto).

Such a feat was not accomplished quickly or easily. He suffered—experiencing losses, broken hearts, deaths, and confusion. According to Cayce, it was a process spanning some thirty incarnations, and hundreds of thousands of years. (I'll share more of the story in the next chapter.) The last of these sojourns was as Jesus of Nazareth.

This is not to say that this great soul has not been on the Earth since that humble, yet profound, life in Palestine, quite the contrary. According to many sources, he continues to enter and help with the ongoing rescue of the lost companions. And according to Cayce, he manifests in the physical world in the same body that he resurrected. He no longer incarnates through birth. Of course, as we already know, this doesn't mean we will immediately recognize him, just as they didn't on the road to Emmaus (Luke 24:13–35). But, let's look at some of his incarnations as he perfected the way.

His first appearance, as Paul indicates (I Cor. 15:45), was as Adam, in which he became a living soul and first experienced physical form, leading to the loss of God's presence and the pain of death. He came again as Enoch, who walked and talked with God. In Adam he was not born of woman but created by God, yet through original sin he came to know death. As Enoch, he was born in the normal way but did not experience death ("God took him," Gen. 5:24).

He appeared again as Melchizedek ("priest of the most high God"), who was neither born nor died, greeting and blessing Abraham in the desert (Gen. 14:18–20). Paul may be indicating his knowledge of this incarnation of Jesus in the following quote from Hebrews.

> Whither the forerunner is for us entered, Jesus, made an high priest for ever after the order of Melchizedek. For this Melchizedek, king of Salem, priest of the most high God, who met Abraham returning from the slaughter of the kings, and blessed him . . . first being by interpretation King of righteousness, and after that also King of Salem, which is, King of peace; without father, without mother, without descent, having neither beginning of days,

> nor end of life; but made like unto the Son of God;
> abideth a priest continually. . . . And it is far more
> evident: for that after the similitude of Melchizedek
> there ariseth another priest, who is made, not after
> the law of a carnal commandment, but after the power
> of an endless life. (Hebrews 6:20–7:16)

Next he came as Joseph, one of the sons of Jacob, and was subjected to all the influences of men and their activities. He did not possess supernatural powers but held fast to his faith that the heavenly Father would be near even in the most desolate places. He was sold by his brothers and taken into the land of the Pharaoh, alone and imprisoned, yet knowing the Father was always aware of him. This belief led to the opportunity to rise to a position of great power and influence by correctly interpreting the dream of the Pharaoh. Eventually Joseph became a savior to his brothers who had sold him away (Gen. 37:23–45:28). This life was a major preparation for his entry as Jesus the Savior.

Even as Jesus he faced tests, first with the three temptations of the devil, and then in the garden, where he struggled with his personal desire not to experience the final test and God's desire that he do so. The last for him to overcome was death. Submission of his will and trust to the will and care of the Father was the way to victory over death. In passing through these tests he gained power over death and oneness with the Father.

To truly comprehend this accomplishment we need to realize that his body was drained of all its natural fluids, blood, and water, and was dead for three days; yet, it came to life again. He walked, talked, and ate (Luke 24:42–43) with this resurrected body.

According to Jesus' own teachings, it is the spirit that gives life, not the flesh. The absence of spirit is physical death and the presence of spirit gives life again, even to a body dead for three days. Lazarus' body had been dead for a week when Jesus called Lazarus' soul to enter it again. For those souls who have come to believe only in the reality of this terrestrial world, these are impossible feats. But once one realizes that one is a spirit and that the spirit lives continuously, then raising the empty three-dimensional vehicle (the body) with the spirit is easy to comprehend—well, easier. However, having knowledge of something and having the power that comes from true understanding of it are two different things. We can hear something and even believe in it, but we will rarely act as though we believe it unless we have personally experienced it.

*Saying* that we are the children of God and the eventual companions of God who have gone astray for a time, and that we are actually celestial beings of spirit, mind, and soul with free will and independent consciousness is all very well, but really *being* such is entirely a different matter. In the experiences of the soul Jesus we can see how all phases of the fall from grace, the struggle with the distracting forces of self's will, the influences of the physical, and the rise again to the original consciousness can be achieved. It happens slowly, patiently, step by step, line upon line, "here a little, there a little" (as the Cayce readings encourage), and before we know it, we are there. This is not thinking or believing we are celestial beings or companions of the Creator, but actually *being* them.

## The Land of Choice

Hundreds of thousands of years have now passed since the companions first entered the Earth. In some ways it must seem as though the rescue has failed. As we look around the planet we still see hundreds of millions of souls who seem to have little awareness of their true nature, their true purpose for living. We see injustice, cruelty, war, violence, all kinds of suffering and deprivation. Yet, in the midst of all of this the rescue continues—quietly, soul by soul. It's as if there were two worlds here on Earth, one focused on the day-to-day activities of the physical planet, with its nations, cities, businesses, races, languages, religions, schools, and endless activities; and another focused on the universal, timeless growth of the souls and their relationship with and awareness of the First Cause, the Creator, the Universal Consciousness. Amid the buying and selling, the building up and tearing down, the fighting and the loving, is a gentle, rising awareness of the brotherhood of all people and a sense of the spirit that survives the material.

There still remains the tendency to seek for solutions among the things of this world when they can only be found within the *inner* place of one's being. It is not outside among the many physical manifestations but within the consciousness of each soul. The physical world is not to be ignored; in fact, it plays a major part in the soul's resurrection, as we shall see.

# 6

## The Lives of Leila: One Soul's Journey

LEILA EVANS DIED when she was only two and a half years old. In view of her short life, we might expect that there isn't much to say about her. Actually, the real story begins with her death. Had she lived, she would have been a close companion of Edgar Cayce's, who incarnated seven months later. The doctors were unable to determine the cause of Leila's death. But her mother knew intuitively that she had slowly drifted away because the family situation had become less than ideal for a little girl, particularly this little girl.

Leila died August 24, 1876. Some sixty years later, in 1936, a young woman walked into the offices of the then aging Edgar Cayce and asked if he would give her one of his now famous readings. Mr. Cayce didn't need to give a reading to know who this woman was—he would have recognized the soul of Leila anywhere—but the subsequent reading served to confirm it. She was indeed the same soul who would have been Cayce's older sister had she not died just months before his birth. The reading intimated that the

souls of Leila and her parents may have made an agreement
with one another prior to her incarnation concerning the
kind of home atmosphere they would have together in their
earthly life. Apparently, the setting was not as agreed upon,
and Leila left. Leila's expectations must have been very
specific and emotionally vital for her to leave a family who
so adored her, for their little angel, according to the readings, was the special one of the family. However, the soul
in the role of the father was not living up to his part of the
plan. His drinking was disrupting this loving family and
ruining Leila's hopes for the new life. The readings then
say, rather cryptically, that she "withdrew to the deeper
meditation in the Mercurian environs."

As mentioned earlier, during the period between physical
lifetimes, souls may experience and learn from the surrounding environments of our solar system, particularly
those of the other planets. They don't actually live *on* the
planets as we do in the third dimension but rather within and
about fourth- and fifth-dimensional environs of these planets. It's as if each planet and star has its unique realm of
experience that attracts souls for specific purposes. Apparently, Leila withdrew to what we might call the fourth dimension of the planet Mercury—not *on* the planet Mercury
but within its fourth-dimensional influences. As we discussed in chapter 3, astrologers have long known that the
planets are far more than just physical spheres in dark space.
Each planet has a special set of characteristics that influence
us. Mercury has astrologically represented the mind. Leila
sought refuge from her disappointment by sojourning there
for, what Cayce called one "full cycle," thirty-three years,
before returning to the environs of Earth to reincarnate on

August 24, 1910—this time under the name of Barbara Murray.

But again her childhood and home setting were lacking in many ways. She was forced to make a decision as to whether she would endure the shortcomings in order to take advantage of the opportunities available through these new parents or withdraw. This time she decided to stay.

It was at the age of thirty that she sat next to the then sixty-year-old Cayce, listening to his description of her soul's life, which seemed to have been going on forever. Remember, had she remained as Leila with her former family incarnation, she would have been his sixty-three-year-old sister. Life is so amazing when viewed from this perspective of the soul. Happily for us, the readings tell of her soul's life from the very beginning, a story that goes something like this. . . .

## A Celestial Child

Leila's soul was conceived in the Mind of God, as were each of us. She was one among many lights that appeared in the dark, as Cayce says, when the "morning stars sang together in the heavens." It was the first dawn and she found herself awake and filled with wonder. In this early morning light her virgin consciousness was so near to the infinite, omnipotent mind of her Creator that the two were as one. Throughout this wondrous Presence were countless others like herself, yet each with a slightly different point-of-being in the whole. They possessed the ultimate combination of consciousness and freedom. And within them were the innate urges of their Creator's desire for companionship and creativity, two celestially primal drives that would remain a driving force forever.

Flush with life, their minds ablaze with wonder and imbued with the essence of their Creator, these fledgling gods began to move, to touch, to seek out and look through the seemingly endless fathoms of the cosmos. As a child would explore everything she found before her, Leila and the others peered into the many and varied mansions of their Father's house. Wonders upon wonders were to be found everywhere their young minds turned.

As with so many of us, Leila's curiosity brought her into the environs of our present solar system. When she arrived here the Earth was still cooling, and life was just beginning to stir in its waters and gases. Her first appearance was not a physical incarnation, for there were no earthly bodies to inhabit as we know them today. Like all companions, she possessed both male and female sexual forces. Her "form" can best be described as a consciousness which could, in moments, be very defined and narrowly focused, and at other times, could expand into the Universal Consciousness and perceive the whole of life. She was a microcosm of the whole, a miniature of her Creator, a "chip off the old block." In this dawn of Earth's life she was like a spirit in the breeze, a voice in the wind as it swept across the steaming waters—a voice foretelling of the coming of man.

But Earth was not the only planet she visited, and the third dimension was not her primary level of consciousness. All the planets in this star system provided her with unique perspectives and opportunities in her young life. The entire universe with its many dimensions was hers to enjoy. By doing so, she would grow in understanding and come to be a true companion to her Creator.

This was Leila in the heavens, long before she made a home in the Earth plane.

## A Terrestrial Child

On one of her early visits to Earth, she and the group of souls with whom she was traveling saw a strangely different quality in many of the souls who had been sojourning near the environs of Earth. They appeared to be changing, becoming more dense and heavy. Their consciousness seemed narrower and less able to expand into the Universal. As she and her companions studied this phenomenon they realized that these souls were gradually moving so deeply into the Earth's dimension that they were separating from the rest of life. They were taking on the characteristics of this new world, and this was causing them to lose awareness of the other dimensions and the higher, finer aspects of their own being. They were no longer just visiting this world; they were actually beginning to look like the animals indigenous to Earth—they had feathers, scales, horns, and other appendages. They were totally new creatures, and communication with them became increasingly difficult.

To her amazement, they had developed a hierarchy among themselves, setting some souls above others, something that was totally alien to the heavenly spheres where they were all children of the same family. These sons and daughters of God had forgotten who they were.

Perhaps the most astonishing change was that the souls who were now leading the terrestrial groups were expounding a belief that there actually was no central, Universal Consciousness to whom they could remain attuned; that in fact their source of life was not a celestial Creator of love and joy, but simply the impersonal force of organic, material life. Each soul was encouraged to take what it wanted from life with little regard for others and none for the whole of life. Successful survivors deserved to live better and off the labor of the others because it would improve the race. Power, superiority, force, strength, and survival of the fittest were among their many new beliefs.

Leila and her companions knew this was nonsense. They reasoned that some great distortion of perception had apparently come over these souls, and in order to see the truth again they needed to regain their finer nature and form. However, in order for Leila and her group to reach them, they were going to have to go deeper into the Earth's dimensions, a move very few of them wanted to make. Yet, they couldn't just leave these lost souls in such a ridiculous state of awareness. After much reflection, Leila and her companions felt sure they could maintain their spiritual consciousness while communicating with these terrestrial ones.

The plan was to first approach those who were the least affected by the Earth's physical dimension. They would reawaken them to the truth and convince them to convey to the others that they were heading in the wrong direction and needed to return to the higher dimensions of life and consciousness.

Though Leila had visited Earth before, this was to be her first sojourn among its unique realms. However, she was not in a body like the ones we occupy today. She and those who came with her made themselves known to the terrestrial souls by projecting images of themselves into the Earth's dimension using light, much in the way we create a hologram. At first Leila's image was much like a sphere of illuminated consciousness, from which her thoughts could be conveyed to the terrestrial souls. But when it became apparent that the terrestrial souls were too three-dimensionally focused to relate to these images, Leila and her companions began to project a form that approached the shape of our bodies today, only much lighter and less dense. It was still very much like a hologram formed by light but with increasing definition.

Using this image form she began to sojourn for the first time in what was to become the continent of Atlantis. Here many souls were living in various degrees of solidity and awareness. Because Leila retained her attunement to the Universal Consciousness, she was considered to be a goddess. Many came to her for guidance and help in understanding what was happening to them and their companions. But she also met with strong, aggressive challenges from the leaders of the terrestrially bound souls. They challenged everything she and her companions held to be true about the Universal One, the higher dimensions, and our true purposes for being.

It quickly became apparent that a transformation in consciousness was going to take much longer than originally expected. The terrestrially possessed companions were far more involved in the Earth than had first been suspected. In fact, many of them were actually seeking to build colonies here and sojourn among the planet's trees, mountains, and waters indefinitely. This might have been completely compatible with the Creator if they had not also been developing an almost idolic interest in themselves and their own desires without any regard for others and the Universal Forces.

## The Children of the Law of One

This self-seeking energy would prove to be the first evil, the first sin. The followers and supporters of the self-centered movement would become known as "the Children of Darkness," because their paths led toward the abyss of separation and loss of contact with the Creator. Prior to these changes there had been only one force. Now there were two; the second, an evil that mounted life for its own purposes, destroying everything in its way. The loss of contact with any holistic source and interconnection to life, combined with the new paradigm reflected in the principles of "survival of the fittest," established an entirely new and inherently destructive dimension of consciousness.

Unfortunately, self-seeking was not the sole possession of the terrestrially bound souls. Every free-willed companion had within it the potential to begin seeking its own way without concern for the effect on others and the whole. Free will and independent consciousness were godly gifts, yet with just the slightest shift in intent these sublime wonders of the fledgling gods became weapons of devils. Each of the companions had to struggle to subdue its self-only desires in order to remain in harmony with the whole and the other companions.

Leila struggled hard to maintain her attunement and to aid those who sought her guidance and counsel, but she could feel herself becoming heavier and assuming more and more of the substance of the Earth. And as she battled with the terrestrial leaders, she found herself becoming more willful and determined to force her views upon them. This righteous and well-meaning desire was subtly giving strength to forces of self-interest, but unlike some of her fellow companions, Leila perceived the effects of willfulness and resisted.

Her name was now Asamee. Hers was not exactly an individual name as we have today; rather, it was the collective name for a line of souls, all of whom were called "Asamee." Individuality was not near what it has become today. Differentiating one soul from another wasn't done; all were still very much one. Those who felt as she did about life and consciousness were called "the Children of the Law of One." This name had come to them because of their insistence that there was only one force in the universe, and souls were the children of the One. They also taught "the Law of the One," which included a principle that actions naturally produce reactions, an idea that the terrestrials considered ridiculous and just another attempt to keep them from doing whatever they wanted.

## The Grand Endeavor

According to the Cayce readings, one of the souls who was with Asamee in these times was called Amilius. This soul would later become known as Jesus of Nazareth. His story weaves in and out of Leila's and is a fascinating one in itself. Cayce said that in these very early times on the planet, Amilius perceived the disastrous change that had come over his fellow souls, resulting in the terrestrial ones, and came to the conclusion that things had gotten beyond the level of a brief flirtation with the Earth. It was now time, he felt, to develop a much more long-term plan for dealing with the situation. On this point, many of the Children of the Law of One disagreed or had other ideas about how to deal with the problem. Thus, for the first time, a difference of opinion arose within the ranks of the Children. Amilius, his intentions pure and his vision clear, was clearly attuned to the Universal Consciousness. Because of this, most of the Children supported his perceptions, some begrudgingly, and others resisted them strongly.

Amilius perceived that if this loss of celestial consciousness could happen to one soul, it could happen to any soul; therefore, the problem needed to be faced; the temptation needed to be overcome. Furthermore, the root of the problem was not the Earth and its unique form of life, but the struggle within each soul to learn to use its godliness in such a way as to be all it was meant to be and yet not destroy itself and other life in the process. Key to this problem was the sense of separation a soul felt as it became more self-conscious and less universally conscious. This sense of separation, which resulted in a loss of purpose and identity with anything or anyone, occurred in the celestial realms as well as in the Earth, though it was more accentuated in the latter. Therefore, it was assumed the Earth was the best place to conquer it.

Amilius was making a commitment to enter the Earth and live among the lost ones in order to help them. He believed that if self-consciousness and its resulting sense of separation could be overcome here, it could be overcome anywhere. And once the earthbound souls saw the truth, the destructive influences would no longer have any power over them and they would be free to fulfill their purpose as companions of God.

Some among Amilius' group wanted to leave the Earthlings to wallow in their own sins and delusions. Others doubted their own ability to resist the temptations that had so possessed the lost souls. For in addition to dealing with the problem of one's own inner temptations and struggles, they were going to have to deal with the terrestrial souls who had now become very aggressive and lawless. To attempt to live among them was not only spiritually, mentally, and emotionally dangerous, it was physically dangerous. Some of the Children also pointed out that there were many complications involved in this Earth problem, a real solution might well be impossible. Perhaps they would just be throwing good souls after bad if they attempted to enter and subdue this world.

With all of these hazards in mind and in spite of much bickering among the Children, Asamee and her fellow souls, including Amilius, began to set up a system whereby the lost ones could regain their heavenly consciousness, and along with the Children of the Law of One, learn to overcome their potential for evil. It was a grand endeavor, filled with the kind of spirit that is only found in the faithful and the hopeful. Little did they know just how formidable their adversary was.

First on their list was to prepare a new physical form that would allow them to sojourn in the Earth with some semblance of their true, spiritual nature. Their animallike forms were totally ill suited for spiritual endeavors and actually added to their problems with perception and understanding. As companions of the Creator, they needed a physical form that suited their particular spiritual characteristics and yet was based on sound principles for functioning well in the third dimension.

Furthermore, their sexual oneness had been eroded by the natural duality of the planet, causing them to accentuate one aspect of their sexual forces (male or female) and subdue the other. No longer were they united, androgynous beings; they were now either predominantly masculine or feminine in their appearance and energy. Physically, then, their new earthly form would need to reflect these changes by being either male or female. Asamee and her fellow "double-sexed" companions began the work of creating male and female forms for these souls by separating their double-sexed natures into single-sexed physical projections. Amilius was the first to completely achieve this.

## The Body of Light

The physical setting for all of these struggles and the subsequent work and commitment was Atlantis. Many souls were involved, and Asamee interacted with most of them, their lives weaving in and out of hers throughout her incarnations. In some cases, they built strong, lasting relationships that were forever a blessing to them. In other cases, they built disagreements, misunderstandings, and distrust that haunted them whenever their paths crossed.

As the work continued, Asamee withdrew from the Earth to prepare herself to be a channel through which the children could enter into the new human bodies. She chose to accentuate her feminine forces and subdue her masculine, and throughout her many incarnations never changed her mind, remaining female in each.

These early periods in the Earth had gone on for an enormously long time. By Earth standards, the activities in Atlantis lasted some 200,000 years. During the last 50,000 years the huge continent had broken into several islands from violent earthquakes. Leila had sojourned here as Asamee for much of the early period and was preparing to return to Earth as the last of Atlantis sank into the sea and a new era began.

This would be her first true incarnation. For this time she was actually going to enter and live in a physical body, a female body. It was not a haphazard event. Many of the souls with whom she had worked in Atlantis were already in the Earth preparing for her arrival.

By now conditions in the Earth had changed dramatically. The rescuing souls had entered en masse in order to prepare for generations of incarnations that were to be a part of this new world. In five different regions, in five different races, in five different nations the souls entered. Each group manifested a unique characteristic of their celestial nature and each was responsible for maintaining and enlightening the physical world with that celestial aspect while the cycles of Earth life moved toward their destiny, or so it was hoped.

Leila, as Asamee, was among those souls charged with developing the white race. Their original center was in the Caucasus Mountains, though many of them migrated into what today would be called northern Africa, Egypt, eastern Asia, and Europe.

In Egypt, the high priest Ra Ta and several others working closely with him were preparing for Asamee's entry.

Hers was to be a very special event, for she had the potential to manifest the optimal characteristics of a true, pure, human-born physical body.

Many of the bodies in all races were contaminated and distorted by animal characteristics that lingered from the early days of the terrestrial ones. To produce a perfect form for the companions, one had to use the natural laws of the Earth's genetics combined with a clear mental image of the desired result. In addition the soul who inhabited the body had to possess the same image and be able to maintain it long enough to manifest it firmly in physical form! Even then, the new creation could end up sexually mingling with another body that wasn't as purely human, mixing it with stronger animal characteristics and ruining everything.

These were unusual times. There were no families, no parents, no laws—just millions and millions of souls in varying degrees of consciousness, with different motives and desires, and different physical bodies. The celestially attuned companions were living in humanlike terrestrial forms, and though their proximity to the lost souls helped awaken many, it also helped to lower the awareness of the celestial ones.

Despite the temptations and difficulties, Ra Ta and his co-workers had prepared themselves and their bodies carefully. They had selected two from their group who were genetically, as well as mentally and spiritually, the best. These beings had been developed, preserved, and finally brought together for the conception of a third body—one that would be even better than the parent bodies.

Asamee had been preparing herself, too. She had sojourned in the celestial environs with as pure an attunement to the Universal One as she could possibly manage. Her connection wasn't as strong as it had been in the first moments after the original creation, where her consciousness was one with all life. Too much had come between her and the deep stillness of the Universal One. But she had maintained a harmony sufficient to make her a rare soul among those who were earthbound, enough for her to show them what it had been like to be a morning star in that now distant dawn.

Ra Ta anxiously watched as the newborn emerged from the womb and as it was cleansed and prepared for presentation. His eyes searched for the telltale signs of beastliness or celestialness and the true characteristics of a pure human form. Again and again he scanned every detail of her body. Nothing, absolutely nothing was distorted or contaminated; she was truly human. Clear sharp eyes, pure skin, very little hair—the priest could hardly believe his eyes. She was the perfect human form for the heavenly souls to use during their incarnations in the new world. It was a time of great joy. As he pulled away to reflect on the meaning and potential of the event, the others who attended the birth pushed their way in to see for themselves.

As mentioned briefly, the celestially aware companions entered the Earth in five different races. This was originally accomplished more in consciousness than in form. Their bodies did not immediately reflect true, pure human qualities but had to be developed over time. At this early stage in man's entry into the Earth, human qualities were more like mental images than physical forms, and in order to convert them into physical reality, it was essential to work within the laws of evolution and genetics native to the Earth.

Ra Ta and his companions had finally achieved the white body. The red had already been perfected, as well as the black; the brown and yellow were near completion. Leila, as Asamee, had been the soul that entered this first purely Caucasian body. Her new name, appropriately, was Tar Ello, "body of light." It was a high achievement for Leila. She gave hope and inspiration to many through her beautiful reflection of one of the five aspects of the heavenly "form." Man was no longer a beast of the world, but a descendant from another world above; a beautiful descendant. Now the work of the ascension was ahead of them, the return to their life "before the world was."

## The Grand Endeavor Fails

Though Tar Ello had accomplished much in achieving her first flesh body, it would prove to be a very difficult incarnation for her. She was looked upon with awe and reverence and viewed and judged by her outer form more than her inner spirit. She naturally felt special, different, and more alone than she had ever felt in the higher dimensions. Even some of her closest companions in the spirit were now so in awe of her that they set her above themselves, no longer swapping counsel and support, but expecting all the wisdom and strength to come from her alone. Others who had been her friends and colleagues in the Atlantian sojourn now resented her new physical superiority, feeling that she no more deserved such an honor than they.

Leila as Tar Ello longed for the early times when no soul was greater than another and all shared together as equals and companions. On Earth everything was measured and judged by appearance, position, and power. It was a lonely place to live, each within one's own body, separated from the others and measured by outer qualities and segregated accordingly.

Tar Ello considered her mission to be above her personal needs and feelings. But Ra Ta perceived the girl's sadness and encouraged her to take part in the ceremonies of the temples and find comfort in prayer and meditation. Ax-Tell and his son Ax-Tellus, both remnants of the Atlantian civilization and members of the perfected red race, had long understood the problems of loneliness and separation in the new world. They knew that Tar Ello and many others were having a difficult time adjusting. And so they encouraged the high priest Ra Ta and the king of the land, Ararat, to consider a new living arrangement for souls while incarnate in the Earth. Instead of living in medium to large groups, their plan was to break them up into small subgroups consisting of one male and one female and their offspring. Together they would form a support group for each of their members, their own flesh and blood the bonding force. It was the beginning of the nuclear family as we know it. This structure would also reflect the heavenly realm where the children of the father-mother God companioned in a close, nurturing environment.

It was an excellent idea, but Tar Ello was a temple virgin, and there was no way Ra Ta was going to agree to allow her to live in a separate dwelling with her natural parents amid all the other souls of mixed blood and morality; this world was still too savage and beastly for that. She was too rare, too special. Tar Ello remained temple priestess, but those close to her knew of her deep longing for companionship and grew concerned. Nevertheless, she struggled hard to maintain her attunement to the Universal One and carried out her daily work to the best of her ability.

She continued to help those around her to make flesh a temporary home for spirit, drawing inspiration and guidance from her temple studies and duties and the many teachers and guides associated with the effort. One of these guides was Hermes, called by many the "Thrice Majestic One." He was, in fact, the soul who had been called Amilius in Atlantis. Continuing his work toward resurrecting the earthbound souls to their former state in the heavens, he was now here in Ancient Egypt among the children who worked toward the same end.

As it is commonly known among the students of ancient mystery today, Hermes was the major influence behind the building of the Pyramids. Since the descent of the souls was going to take them deep into the world of matter and physical reality, these monuments were built as reminders of the former realms that still lie beyond physical death. But they were more than monuments in those early days. Leila as Tar Ello and her fellow Children of the One used some of these structures for their initiations into the true realities and purposes for life, truths that were fast becoming myths and legends. Through her close relationship with Ra Ta and his close relationship with Hermes, she continued to be involved with this great soul and his destiny.

Unfortunately, after the death of Ra Ta, who had become her inspiration and strength, Tar Ello fell from the high pedestal she had so sincerely accepted. Eventually, she left the temple to become the companion of Exderenemus, another soul from the time of Atlantis and one with whom she would companion in many of her incarnations.

These dramatic changes in Tar Ello's life and position astonished those who worshipped her and caused those who resented her to take every opportunity to discredit her. All of this left Leila's soul deeply distressed. What had begun as a grand endeavor was ending in a purposeless mess. She withdrew from her body, from this place of sadness, and sought to rid herself of the memory of the whole experience. She sojourned in the realms of Saturn, and cleansed herself of all remnants of the flesh. From Saturn she withdrew even further from Earth, her spirit rising higher and higher until she could feel the light of the Universal One fill her being and purge her of her earthly dross. Here in the heavenly spheres she bathed and rejuvenated herself until once again she and her Creator were in touch with each other.

## The Holy Land

As Earth keeps time, it wasn't long before the soul of the priest Ra Ta and those of Leila's other companions beckoned her to join them in another visit to the environs of Earth and yet another attempt at helping the terrestrially bound souls reawaken themselves. It was too much a part of Leila's deepest wishes for her to refuse this goodwill mission, and because the Earth afforded her the opportunity to mend her disappointing life in Egypt, she readily accepted the challenge. Off she went, revitalized and ready to make things right.

Together with her little band of like-minded souls, Leila

lived through many, many lifetimes in the Earth and in the realms beyond. Members of her loose-knit group were not always in agreement with one another or even considerate to one another, but, like most families, they were a unit, even a team at times. One of their most significant incarnations came during the time of Christ.

In this incarnation Leila and Ra Ta were brother and sister. Her name was Nimmuo and his was Lucius. Both were prominent members of the church at Laodicea. They lived in the Holy Land during the occupation of the Roman Legions. That particular portion of Asia had been under the control and supervision of the Roman Empire for a very long time; their presence and power permeating every aspect of life in these regions.

Nimmuo's father was of Roman descent and had two wives, one Grecian and one Jewish. Nimmuo was the child of the Greek mother while her brother Lucius was the son of the Jewish mother. Since the Romans always made attempts to put in authority any locals who showed sympathy for the needs and demands of the Empire and who could be helpful in making activities with the local people more harmonious, her Roman-born father and, therefore, the entire family, enjoyed the support of Rome. For very practical reasons the armies of Rome did not want trouble with the people they conquered; they simply couldn't afford to keep expending any more of their resources governing these distant lands. And so Nimmuo's family was given many financial and personal freedoms that were rare in those times. Her father, with his Jewish wife and close connections with the Jewish churches in the north, was considered to be of great benefit to the Empire so that even their Jewish church profited.

Nimmuo and her family held tightly to the tenets and morals of their Hebrew faith, and though they interacted with the Roman leaders, they shunned the lewdness and immorality the Romans brought to the Holy Land.

As the activities and teachings of Jesus reached their homeland in the North, the family began to come under their influence. To the Children of the Law of One, Jesus' teachings were a balm to their weary souls and a beacon pointing the way to a forgotten consciousness and life. They knew that his blossoming ministry abruptly changed during the periods of Jesus' trial and the Crucifixion. And then subsequent reports spread across the land about his rising again three days after dying on the cross and meeting with the disciples at the Sea of Tiberius. When news of this miraculous event reached their ears, the entire family was caught up in wonderment and interest.

So Nimmuo, then barely sixteen years old, and her brother, who was now a leading minister in their church, set off to the South to learn everything they could. Nimmuo wanted to meet and talk with everyone who had come in contact with the Master. Because she and her brother traveled under the protection and support of the Romans, many along the way were skeptical of their true faith and loyalty to Israel and the Master's teachings. However, the people they visited perceived the sincerity and faithfulness of these two northerners. Their suspicion turned to trust and they shared with Nimmuo and Lucius the many stories about the Master's life and teachings.

They journeyed through the Holy Land, across the Sea of Galilee, down to those lands in Jordan through Perea to Bethany and the house of Martha, Mary, and Lazarus, and then into the City of Jerusalem itself. They met Mary, the Mother of Jesus, and the rest of the family that had gathered under John's roof as he had been instructed from the Cross.

In Bethany they heard the story about Mary Magdalene's cleansing from her sins and Martha's devotion and tireless efforts to care for everyone's needs. Straight from Lazarus himself they heard about his death and his feelings and consciousness during the four days that his dead body lay in the tomb. He told them what it was like in the realms between Earth life and Spirit life, and how he had heard and felt the movement within himself when the Voice called, "Lazarus, come forth!"

All this affected Nimmuo to her very soul, making contact with those old sensations when she had been so close to her Creator and leaving an imprint on her soul memory for eternity.

## A Soul's Finest Hour

As they traveled on they continued to hear reports of how people had been healed by the laying on of his hands or merely his word spoken, how they had eaten bread that had been created by the word of the Teacher. Nimmuo and her brother were kept in rapt attention over and over again and they were forever changed by all they learned.

However, these times of enlightenment and awakening were not to pass peacefully. The Romans began to move against this growing new group that they considered to be nothing more than troublemakers. Nimmuo was present at one such event when James, the brother of Jesus, was chosen as head of the new church along with Peter. She witnessed how the other James, one of the Apostles, and his brother, John, the sons of Zebedee, had so stirred the spirit of the crowds that the Romans became afraid of the mass meeting and attacked with swords drawn. They killed John's brother and many others during the riot and eventually exiled John to Patmos. These two sons of Zebedee had long been called "the sons of thunder," and the Romans had had enough of them. From this moment on the followers of the humble Nazarene would be persecuted by the authorities.

With the scattering of the disciples and friends, Nimmuo and her brother returned to Laodicea and the other churches of the North. They both grew in power and position because of their travels, knowledge, and understanding about the great events of these times. Deep within Nimmuo she felt the essence of the many things she had heard in the homes of Mary, Martha, Lazarus, and the Mother. As so often in her previous lives, her soul yearned for the Spirit, for the soothing sense of the Divine Presence that she had always loved. Now, amid all the daily activities of this world and its limited perspective on life, she applied herself to the work that had begun many thousands of years earlier in that lost and forgotten land of Atlantis.

Remember, everyone with whom she presently associated had been involved with her in Atlantis and Egypt and in several lifetimes in between. Amilius, who had remained so attuned to the Universal Consciousness during his life in Atlantis that he committed himself to the rescue of the lost souls, was the very person they now called Jesus. In this Divine Incarnation he had prepared the final phase of salvation for all earthbound souls. He and the heavenly Father were one throughout this life, not separate. It was seen by all who could still perceive with their spiritual, celestial eyes that reunion with the Creator was possible, thereby making it easier for others to follow.

Nimmuo was one who saw the truth, and the stories she heard on her journey through Jesus' homeland filled her soul with a new fervor and determination to continue with the work. Along with her brother and many others, she ministered to the needs of the people, particularly those involved in the church at Laodicea. And when the church was nearly destroyed from within by a severe difference of opinion on how best to judge what was right and what was wrong, Nimmuo's serene and patient counsel kept the church from dividing. She seemed to sense the inner meaning of the teachings and never got lost in the many surface interpretations and dogmas in which man so often becomes tangled.

This was not an easy time for Nimmuo. She was surrounded by the very same souls who had seen her fall in Egypt, and many of them doubted her new-found inspiration, suspecting she would once again let them down. But they underestimated her determination to make things right with all these souls she had once failed. This was her opportunity, and she seized it, snatching victory from out of the mouth of defeat. Using all the wisdom and strength within her, she rose to the occasion, and many other souls rose a little higher because of her. These were her soul's finest hours.

She lived a long and fulfilling life and withdrew to the peace of the heavenly environs for a lengthy period of meditation, letting the truths of that incarnation permeate deeply into her consciousness. She was a far wiser child of God than the one who taught in Atlantis. She had seen the face of the beast and tamed it, at least most of it. But there was a little more yet to deal with, as she would soon see.

## Reunited

After sojourning in the heavens for many Earth years, the soul of Leila returned for an incarnation that was most uncharacteristic. The Earth was now a major center of physical activity and was densely populated. All of life and the universe were now viewed almost totally from a physical perspective. The biological history of the Earth established and supported the narrow concept of physical reality, and nearly everyone accepted it as the only reality. Business and commerce, religion and government, love and money had all become the powerful structures in which most lived. Into this world, so very different from the earlier ones, the soul of Leila incarnated as the daughter of a wealthy and prominent Englishman. Her name was Marge Olglethorp. She learned her role well and even enjoyed it. Parasols, long, whirling hoop skirts, fancy buggies, and parties with all kinds of foods and beverages were the style of the day. Life was just a bowl of cherries, ripe for eating and enjoying. Amazingly, Leila, as Marge, took to this fun little lifetime quite well. No great mission beyond pomp and pleasure, no great challenges to overcome beyond style and good taste—life was to be lived to its fullest.

On one of the family's journeys to America, Marge found herself caught up in the role of being a southern belle and was well received by the ladies and gentlemen of this land of willows and moss, huge plantations, and wealth beyond measure. Here she lived the life of a Georgia peach, with that special touch of breeding that is forever English. Ra Ta was not involved in this lifetime, but Exderenemus, her husband in Ancient Egypt, was. In fact, he had incarnated with her life as Nimmuo, but the two of them did not develop a close relationship. In the present incarnation in England and Southern America a terrible disagreement ended their relationship with such bitterness that they would of necessity face it again in a future incarnation.

How did this carefree lifetime become part of the experience of a soul who was once the goddess of Atlantis, the perfection of Ancient Egypt, and a minister at Laodicea? The Eastern teachings of reincarnation include a concept that souls live a carefree life about every six incarnations—a vacation, if you will, from the main work of spiritual resurrection. Perhaps the soul of Leila was enjoying a much needed break from her many serious lifetimes of devotion, trial, and hard lessons learned.

It was after her incarnation as Marge that she reincarnated as Leila Cayce, which brings us back to the beginning of our story. Subsequently she reincarnated as Barbara Murray, the woman who found herself sitting that day some thirty years later next to the "sleeping prophet," Edgar Cayce. Barbara was a serene, elegant woman who devoted much of her time and energy to the work of Edgar Cayce, who, not surprisingly, was the reincarnation of the soul who had been Ra Ta in Ancient Egypt and her brother Lucius in the Holy Land. In the present lifetime, Barbara married Exderenemus again, now called Ryan Simons. The Cayce reading warned them not to let this relationship end like it had in their previous life together. Amilius was now their

Christ, having become one with the Father again and resurrected to prepare a place for them and each and every one
of us. The three of them, Barbara, Ryan, and Edgar Cayce,
had long ago dedicated themselves to this soul they had
known so closely throughout his lifetimes and his earthly
mission. They continued to live and teach the mystery that
we are all celestial beings descended from our original heavenly kingdom through a long and arduous journey in this
realm of physical reality and destined to return from whence
we came.

# PART TWO

Reincarnation Today

# 7

## Past Lives and Present Relationships

WE ARE LIKE rivers. On the surface we are all shiny and clear, shimmering with freshness and life, but deep within us run powerful unseen currents of soul memories and desires. These deep currents are the cumulative effects of ages of soul life and many incarnations in the Earth. They cause us to love one person and despise another, to feel wonderful vibrations with a particular individual in one area of our lives and to feel awkward and uncomfortable with that same person in another part of our lives. Patterns and habits have formed deep within our inner-consciousness and shape the ways we interact with people around us.

Everyone involved in our *present* lives was very likely involved in our *past* lives. Actually, it is likely they have been involved in *many* of our past lives. Our parents, brothers and sisters, spouses, children, friends, colleagues, bosses and employees, and even our enemies began sharing life with us long before the present lifetime.

The effects of these many past-life experiences are reflected in the circumstances that now surround our present relationships. The soul's memories of past-life activities with others shape our innate reactions to them. Of course, *their* memories of our past-life actions influence how they react to us as well. Through the same eyes that the personality sees life, the soul sees it, but the soul looks with a memory covering centuries of passion and adventure, caring and love, hatred and revenge, doubt and fear. When we feel a seemingly unfounded fondness for another person, it is very likely due to a soul memory of the positive role he or she played in our past lives. On the other hand, when we react with what seems to be an unfounded revulsion or hatred toward another person, we can be pretty sure it is because the soul recalls their past actions against us or our loved ones.

However, the influences of past-life actions are rarely so clear cut. Often those with whom we have had many good lives and relationships are the same people with whom we have had many problems and disagreements, a mix of good and bad karma, so to speak. The positive, well-developed aspects from our past lives will give us much pleasure and support in the present, and those with which we had difficulties will give us opportunities for growth and understanding in present relationships. Avoiding these influences is simply not possible. Whether we like it or not, the Universal Law of Karma constantly brings before each of us the meeting of our past use of free will and consciousness. Thus, what we have done to other souls and they have done to us is reflected in the circumstances surrounding our present interactions and the basic, innate urges, attitudes, and emotions we feel toward each other.

## Soul Groups

The underlying principles of past relationships and their present influences are true of group relationships as well. From the beginning our souls have tended to travel together in clusters, and over time this has created forces of attraction that help to maintain and build on these group relationships. Nearly all souls on the planet today were together in past ages of human history. As a result, the relationships among the peoples of the world today are a reflection of their past activities with each other.

The souls who came in to our planetary system and entered the realms of consciousness associated with it comprise the largest soul group. This group can be divided into subgroups called "the generations," containing souls who move through the natural cycles of Earth life together. These can then be divided into the various nations, cultures, races, religions, etc., that have formed during ages of interaction with each other. Within these there are still other subgroups of souls who share similar philosophies, ideas, purposes, aspirations, and attitudes. And these can be further divided into the many smaller groups of personal relationships: communities, families, businesses, teams, schools, and so on.

Soul groups create an affinity among their members based on the cumulative experiences they share and through their collective memory of how life has been for them and what they have come to mutually desire out of it. In a manner of speaking, such groups form a distinct collective consciousness and spirit, much like the souls who gave us "the spirit of '76," reflecting that group's mutual hopes, attitudes, purposes, and memories.

Those who belong to one soul group can move to another if they desire. Any individual soul can use its free will to seek an experience in a different group. There are many cases of souls changing political allegiance, race, or religion from one lifetime to another. Neither do the generations incarnate in strict, rigid patterns. A member of one generation may enter again with another generation. For example, two members of a family who were father and son in one life may change positions and become son and father in another, or grandfather and grandson. They may even choose to be in the same generation in an incarnation as brothers. However, they may also choose not to be in the same family again.

Although soul groups are fairly well established and have significant pull on the individuals within them, they do not have greater influence than an individual soul's will to change.

Generally, however, soul groups cycle in and out of the Earth together and, therefore, at approximately the same time. (I am speaking in eras and ages, not days or years.) This is particularly evident in the past-life readings given by Edgar Cayce. Many of them were for souls who fell into one of two major soul groups and naturally followed their cycles of incarnation. Sometimes both groups were in the Earth during the same periods but in different locations. Edgar Cayce and those who worked closely with him also traveled with one of these two groups.

THE INCARNATIONS OF TWO MAJOR SOUL GROUPS
FOUND IN THE EDGAR CAYCE READINGS

**Group 1:**
>   Early Atlantis
>   Early Ancient Egypt
>   Persia (during the time of Croesus I, II)
>   Palestine (during the time of Christ)
>   The Crusades
>   Colonial America

**Group 2:**
>   Late Atlantis
>   Late Ancient Egypt
>   Early Greece
>   Rome (during the time of Christ)
>   France (during the time of Louis XIV, XV, XVI)
>   The American Civil War

Of course, this list represents only the most significant incarnations for these souls. They probably have incarnated many more times than shown here, but the majority of the readings were for souls who typically cycled with one of these two major groups. Cayce indicated that there were exceptions to this pattern, and we should take a brief look at them as well.

As mentioned earlier, some souls did not stay together throughout every lifetime. They chose instead to skip a cycle or enter with a different cluster, though they usually rejoined their original group eventually. Others, though cycling into the Earth plane with their group, did not actually physically incarnate. They did not enter into a body but stayed in the spirit and helped from a higher vantage point while the others incarnated. One example of this comes from an Edgar Cayce reading for a woman who wanted to know why she hadn't been given an incarnation during the Palestine era in which her present son and husband had lived. She was told that she was there, but not in the flesh. She was, as some of us would term it today, a "guardian angel" for her present son while he lived and worked in that period.

A group of souls may find themselves together again and yet not one of them desired it to be so. In these cases, it is often the forces of the Universal Law that cause them to come together. For better or for worse they now have to meet the effects of their past actions with each other. The Universal Intention is that the confrontation will lead to a resolution of their karma or at least a recognition of how their past actions with each other have caused the present predicament, and they will resolve not to act that way again.

Both in individual and group relationships, the karmic effects of past actions with others can create some very difficult, even terrible situations. The meeting can result in murder, rape, torture, and other atrocities. Even in lesser cases karmic effect can result in backbiting, backstabbing, bickering, fighting, and other turmoils. Imagine what might happen if the universal forces of cause and effect brought together the souls of the Roman Coliseum and the souls they fed to the lions, or the Conquistadors and the Incas and Aztecs, or the Nazis and Jews.

The same cause-and-effect forces play a part in individual lives, too. Imagine if the Universal Law brought together a victim killed in a family quarrel and his or her murderer. What about a soul who betrayed another's trust or love? What would be the reaction toward one another in this present life? When lives are heavily burdened by the negative effects of their past actions, their present experience is often tragic, and occasionally their lives may appear to be wasted senselessly. However, from the soul's perspective a single incarnation is a learning experience and an opportunity to resolve past actions that are now holding the soul back from a fuller life. One physical life is not the ultimate living experience for the soul. It is an opportunity to resolve the burdens past actions have placed upon our souls and to clear away the many ideas that continue to confuse and limit us. So even though the seventy or eighty years that comprise the average lifetime seem so very singular and final, it is only a temporary sojourn, a brief experience along an infinite path of soul life.

Of course, all the good that has been experienced among the various souls and soul groups has just as strong an effect on present situations as does evil, and when we focus on this good karma we often find better ways to resolve the negative influences.

## The Bond of Soul Mates

A soul mate is really nothing more than a soul or souls (and there may be several of them) with whom we have *closely* shared so many lifetimes that we now resonate to the same pitch, so to speak. We understand each other like no one else can. This kind of history gives soul mates the capacity to help each other in ways that would be difficult without the deep bonding that has occurred through the ages.

Soul mates often assist each other in reaching their

highest potential. Although each of them will still have to apply himself to making the present relationship the best it can be, their deep inner knowing of the other gives them a distinct advantage. However, being soul mates doesn't automatically mean that they see eye to eye on everything. They are usually more like complements than duplicates of each other. Each one brings to the union something the other is missing, thereby rounding out the relationship and giving each of them more than they would have separately.

When soul mates are together, they form a dynamic bond and provide a source of strength that is very hard to find in our world. They may presently be in either sex and interact with each other in any number of relationships. There is a strong tendency to think of soul mates only in the sense of love and marriage, but they can also be partners, parents, siblings, teammates, friends, etc. Having been lovers and mates in many past lives, however, it would be very hard for them to avoid at least a romantic interlude in the present life. There may simply be too much magnetism for them to easily ignore each other and the physical attraction. If, on the other hand, they had been close friends or family members throughout their incarnations, they would be inclined toward a similar relationship in the present. The point is, a soul mate is not always a sexual mate.

Another important point about soul mates is that the true mate of every soul is its Original Companion, the Creator, who gave each of us life for the very purpose of being eternal companions with him. As far as the sexual dynamics of soul mating, it's important to keep in mind that in the heavenly home we (our souls) "neither marry nor are given in marriage." As souls, we are actually siblings in the Universal Family. Therefore, even though soul mates may give each other the support that is needed and deserved in this difficult world—which may include healthy, intimate, sexual companionship—they are ultimately brothers and sisters in the spiritual realms.

## Duality and Twin Souls

This brings us to one of the strangest concepts concerning soul relationships, that of "Twin Souls." As we have already seen, a soul possesses both the male and female forces within itself prior to entering the duality of the Earth. As the soul enters the world it usually selects one of its two sexual natures and projects the unique characteristics of this sex while incarnate. As difficult as it may be to understand, the unmanifested sexual part of our soul can actually incarnate at the same time we do. In other words, our soul, which is much more complex than we have imagined, is capable of dividing its dual sexual nature into two separate and distinct entities, one male and the other female. Each of these two entities can incarnate into the Earth at the same time in separate bodies that usually complement the present sex. That is to say that somewhere out there in the physical world is literally our other half—the other sexual aspect of our soul!

Fortunately, there are some examples of this in the Cayce readings. One of the more notable is a group of four souls who, in their present incarnation, were husband, wife, eldest son, and a female business associate who was also a very close friend of the family. The husband was told through Cayce readings that his present wife was his soul mate and that his life would never have reached its fullest potential without her. However, it went on to say that the female business associate and close friend of the family was his "twin soul"; in other words, she was the other sexual half of his complete soul. Furthermore, his wife's twin soul was their eldest son! I realize how bizarre all of this sounds, but the dynamics and dimensions of life are simply far greater than we imagine. Of course, not all examples are as closely knit.

Generally, the twin soul relationship is presently found among spouses, friends, occasionally as parent and child. Sometimes the twin soul isn't even incarnate at the same time. However, there does seem to be a pattern that most twin soul relationships follow. In their early incarnations together they tend to be mates or at least seek a lover's relationship with each other. In later incarnations they tend to seek less sexually involved relationships and more work-related activities together, especially when the work has a soul purpose. This could be due to the process we reviewed earlier where, in the period of the souls' descent into materiality, they tended to continue their self-seeking, self-satisfying pursuits. But on the ascent toward a return to spirituality they tended to seek more holistic purposes and relationships. That is not to say that all present sexual relationships are self-seeking. From the Cayce material we find healthy support for marriage and home and all the natural sexual aspects that are a part of the union of two in love and mutual caring.

## Parents and Children

As difficult as it may be for us to believe, each soul actually chooses its parents—with one exception. If a soul has abused its gift of free will, then it comes under the strong influence of the Universal Law and is carried along on the force of its past actions into present relationships that it simply must face up to. Of course, no soul is given more than it can handle, not that it won't suffer. But it won't be totally lost or destroyed by the burdens of its karma. Generally, however, a soul chooses its parents prior to entering the Earth.

As we would expect, souls who have had experiences together in past lives will have a stronger attraction for one another than souls who have had no past experiences together. Even if souls aren't particularly fond of one another they still tend to be drawn together by the force of their past interaction. Furthermore, if the soul has a specific purpose for incarnating, and most of us do, then it will be seeking others who are a part of fulfilling its purpose or those who can at least contribute to it. Again, this doesn't mean that the childhood family life will be all hugs and kisses. In every relationship we can find advantages and disadvantages, and in order to enjoy one we must accept the other. In fact, in many cases the disadvantages lead to or create the opportunities for the advantages. When a soul is trying to decide which channels (parents) would be best for it to enter this world, it has to accept the limitations of the particular family as well as the opportunities.

From the spiritual realm Earth life appears much like a river when viewed from high above. The soul who is deciding which channels to enter through sees the river in all its vastness, with many tributaries and branches, and it sees where the parents' boat is on the river of life. In this way it has an overview of what life will be like with these parents. However, because the river has many side routes, the incoming soul can only see the strongest current in the parents' lives. It can't be sure that one of the free-willed parents won't change its mind and begin pursuing a different course or that the currents themselves won't shift and thereby change the family's future. It can't even be certain that it won't change its own mind once it gets into the boat.

Destiny and fate do exist, and they exist side by side with free will. The effects of our past actions have an inertia that carries over into the present life and shapes it, thereby creating our destiny. However, nothing surpasses the power of the soul's divinely given free will. At any time we can use our will to change directions, change attitudes, change purposes, change anything! In this way, our lives are both fatalistically foreshadowed by the cause-and-effect forces of our past use of free will and yet amenable to change by our present use of free will. Therefore, the incoming soul can see only the general course of the family's riverboat; it can't be sure the family will stay the course.

The incarnate parents also have significant influence as to which soul enters through them. Their daily thoughts, desires, and purposes create a beacon for souls who respond to these energies. This is particularly true of the mother. Her daily activities and inner thoughts during the gestation period create a field much like a magnet. As you would expect, more than one soul may be attracted to the same mother-to-be. In such cases, the forces of cause and effect, the will power and desire of the mother, and the souls wanting to incarnate combine to make the selection. The souls who were not chosen for the present entry may well come in through a later pregnancy if the opportunity is presented. Or they may go on to other families with whom friendships or other blood relationships would naturally form and be maintained with the original channel family.

The soul generally enters the infant's body at or near the time of birth. In one unusual case in the Cayce readings, the soul did not enter for two days after the birth of the baby. When asked about the delay, Cayce responded that the soul was all too aware of how difficult life would be should it choose to enter, and it wasn't at all sure it wanted to go through with it! Cayce was then asked what kept the baby's body alive for two days while the soul wrestled with its decision, and he responded, "the spirit." For Cayce, the soul was the entity, with all its personal memories and aspirations, and the spirit was the life force.

According to the metaphysical work of Rudolf Steiner, the soul actually incarnates in four stages: A first level of consciousness enters at or near the time of birth; a second and greater level of consciousness enters around the time the child cuts its first teeth; a third level enters during puberty; and the final and complete entry of the soul occurs close to the age of twenty-one.

Most sources agree that the first couple of years of life are primarily devoted to developing the physical body and that the years from two to seven shape much of the child's sense of self and its view of the world. In addition to the well-known physical and emotional changes that occur during the course of puberty, Cayce and other metaphysical sources add that this is the time when *karmic* influences begin to take hold, coinciding with the release of hormones. This perspective sheds so much light on the otherwise baffling or incomprehensible changes in personality and behavior that sometimes accompany this stage of physical development. Around the age of twenty-one the individual begins to assume its major course through life. From here on the life progresses through a series of experiences and decision crossroads. These occur in natural and identifiable cycles, the most influential being the seven-year cycle: one through seven, eight through fourteen, fifteen through twenty-one, twenty-one through twenty-eight, and so on. Notice how these cycles coincide with the general metaphysical cycles of birth, seven years of age, puberty (though puberty usually occurs before age fourteen, it is fulfilled at or near this age), and twenty-one years of age.

Furthermore, each soul experiences life in two primary arenas: the inner world of self, which includes one's mental and emotional being and physical body; and the outer arena of life's unique circumstances, including the social, economic, racial, national, and religious environment, all of which are generally set at birth.

## Past-Life Readings

In order for us to really understand how all of this occurs and what it means in our own lives, let's look at some real-life examples.

Like most young girls, Linda Mills wanted to fall in love with a wonderful man, have a family, and live a rich, full life. When she met her future husband, she was genuinely attracted to him, though she knew he wasn't everything she had dreamed about. She especially didn't like his tendency to make decisions for her. Nevertheless, their love for each other was strong and they felt a deep mutual attraction.

They married and had two daughters. For Linda, the first daughter was a joy. Throughout the pregnancy and after the birth she and her new baby were very comfortable and happy with each other. They spent many wonderful hours together nursing and rocking while Linda softly hummed lullabies. But life with her second daughter was quite a different story. The pregnancy was uncomfortable, filled with sickness and stress, and after the birth she and the baby just never seemed to get into sync with each other. The baby didn't seem to enjoy being held or rocked like the first child and breastfeeding was a battle. In fact, the baby developed an allergy from the breast milk, and formula had to be substituted. Only the father's touch was comforting to this little one, and as she grew up her preference for him became even more evident. She was clearly "Daddy's little girl," while the first child was certainly Mommy's.

When this family received a past-life reading from Edgar Cayce, the cause of many of their present feelings and actions quickly surfaced. Apparently, Linda and her husband had been husband and wife before, but in the incarnation just prior to this one, they had been father and daughter, respectively. His tendency to make decisions for her and control her life was a carryover from then. In that past life

Linda had been a rather wild and rebellious child. This was due in part to her resentment that the man who had been her equal in many lifetimes was now her father. It was a difficult life for him, too. Raising her was very hard, especially after the death of his wife in that lifetime. Naturally, all of these feelings carried over into their present life and marriage.

As for the children, the first daughter had been Linda's close friend through many lifetimes, bringing this love and friendship into the present life. In their most recent past life, the first daughter had helped Linda deal with the problems Linda had had with her father (Linda's present husband), and now as their daughter she would do so again. The second daughter had been the father's lover in many past lives, so you can just imagine the mutual enmity this created between the mother and daughter in the present. Linda's milk wasn't *all* the baby was allergic to! Neither did she want Linda's love and comfort as much as she did her father's. The father and his second daughter would have to learn to love each other in a much different way or break one of the strictest taboos, incest. All of these feelings were occurring subconsciously, of course, subtly affecting the conscious life.

As we can see, the deep currents of past experiences were playing a significant role in their present relationships. According to the Cayce readings, their goal now, from their souls' point of view, was to live together again and make an effort to accentuate the love and virtues, and minimize the resentments and bad habits they carried with them as a result of their past.

In another case, despite all his efforts to ignore or resist it, Michael Parks was afraid of the dark. His fear was not like most children's; he was *deathly* afraid, to the point of suffocating if left in the dark too long. As far as he and his parents could recall, his childhood was rather normal and nothing had occurred that might have caused this reaction. Yet, during his childhood, anyone in charge of him had to be aware of his fear and take precautions to insure that he was never inadvertently left alone in a dark room or house. His parents were unusually understanding and sympathetic of his need. And later, when he married and started a family of his own, his wife assumed the burden of his fear. She too proved to be very patient with him. Together they worked out an elaborate scheme whereby he could go to bed with the lights on and she would come to bed after he had fallen asleep. Only then would she turn the lights off. Even so, if he awoke during the night, he would become extremely anxious and uncomfortable. He would have to fight to keep himself from panicking before turning on his bedside light. But once the light was on, the only way he could get back to sleep was to go into the living room, turn on all the lights, and sleep on the couch.

One night Michael awoke from a terrifying dream, a dream that was to be the beginning of his conquering the fear. He dreamed that he was in a dark dungeon surrounded by wet stone walls that went up so high he couldn't see where they ended. There was absolutely no way out and no one was coming to help him. As he stood there he began to cry. He cried so long and hard that the cell began to fill with his tears. When he noticed the tear water was up to his chest, he tried to stop crying but couldn't get hold of himself.

He felt completely trapped without hope of ever seeing light or life again. Eventually, the pool of tears reached his nose and he had to stand on his tiptoes to breathe, yet he continued to cry. Slowly he allowed himself to ease under the water, drifting into a sorrowful, lonely dream of letting go, surrendering his will to the reality of his predicament. At this point he awoke from the dream. The sheets were soaked, and his body was covered with chilly sweat. When he told his wife and parents the dream they cried and were very upset by it. However, underneath Michael was beginning to feel pretty good. In fact, he noticed his fear of the dark had actually diminished since the dream. It was as though something in that dream had healed and changed him.

About a year later Michael happened to take part in a series of exercises for recalling past-life experiences. From the information he received during these exercises and several more dreams over the next two years, he began to understand why he was afraid of the dark.

In a previous incarnation he had been a renegade from the courts and causes of Louis XIV. So violent and disruptive were his counterattacks against the king that he became one of the most wanted men in France. His raids destroyed many of the king's storehouses, and his ability to elude capture created a great deal of hatred among the king's soldiers. One day they did capture him. In retaliation for his actions and also as a result of their frustration with trying to stop him, they threw him into the bottom of a well-like dungeon, covered it, and left him there to die a slow death.

In this terrible place of complete darkness, he managed to survive for several days. In the beginning he was sure his friends and his wife would rescue him. But as time went by he realized that no one was coming and he gave up hope and died. In the latter days of his ordeal he lost all sense of time and his mind began to fall apart. He could no longer be sure of what was real and what was illusion. But the worst part was the unrelenting darkness and confinement. This was what his soul remembered and most feared.

Just as we might expect, his current parents and wife, who helped him deal with his fear in the present life, had been the very people he had counted on to rescue him from the dungeon. His father and his wife had been his close friends and colleagues-in-arms, while his present mother had been his wife in the French incarnation. They didn't go to his rescue because he had become so notorious that they probably would have been captured and thrown into the dungeon with him. To a great degree, his own actions had brought him to this end, yet his parents and wife regretted that they had not at least tried to save him. His present-life dream was too much for his parents and wife to hear without deeply reacting to his ordeal. However, Michael's reliving the experience in his dream somehow released him from his life-long fear of the dark.

In yet another less dramatic case, a man who had fallen in love with a divorcée found himself struggling with his feelings. He eventually married her and tried to be a good stepfather to her child. But when he discovered that he could not father children himself, he felt cheated and fought feelings of resentment toward the special relationship between his wife and her child. When he received a past-life reading from Edgar Cayce, he was told that in a previous incarnation in ancient Greece he had been married to the same woman. In that life she was the one unable to conceive a child. Though aware of her sadness and heightened sensitivity because of the added implications of being barren in those days, he chose a second wife to bear him a child. He further shamed and humiliated her by bringing the second wife and child to live in the same house, forcing her to witness the open joy and affection expressed in the little family. In his present-life circumstances, according to Cayce, he was merely meeting himself. Though he deeply desired his own offspring, he was sterile; and though living in his own home, he felt like an outsider to the love shared within it.

Taking advantage of the present situation and making life as miserable as possible for her husband would simply be setting herself up for a future destiny of sadness. The law of karma is very impersonal: what one does one experiences, without exception. If this woman now chose to help her husband meet his fate as best she could, she would heal many wounds and free herself at the same time.

In still another case, a beautiful woman from the modern cosmopolitan life of a big city came to Cayce and described her tragic predicament, asking for a remedy. Her present husband was impotent, and she was a beautiful woman in the prime of her life. Why? Why was she in such a tragic situation? she lamented. She went on to say that there was another man she knew at work, and she wondered if she could have an affair with him yet remain with her husband. She loved her husband, but she wanted to fulfill all of her womanhood. Cayce responded by showing her why she was faced with such a dilemma.

In a past incarnation during the Crusades, she and her present husband had also been married to each other. He was then one of the greatest of the Crusaders, often going off to war. However, every time he left, he saw to it that she wore a chastity belt, literally putting her under lock and key! Then and there she swore deep in her heart she would get even with him. Now, Cayce said, she had him right where she'd always wanted him—in a position where she could make him pay dearly.

What a triangle! I wouldn't be surprised if the other man had also been hanging around the castle while the rest of the Crusaders were off to war. At any rate, here they were again, set up perfectly to play out resolution or revenge for past actions with each other. The husband had used his free will to squash his wife's, forcing her to submit to his sexual restraints without any choice on her part. Now he found himself sexually restricted and frustrated and completely subject to her will and her choices. *She* now had the power to make *him* pay. What a tangled web. The choice to make this right was completely hers; nothing was standing in her way.

Cayce advised her to do whatever she would want done to her if she were in her husband's shoes, and she did. She withdrew from the other man's affections and built a loving home with her husband. No doubt she will eventually incarnate into a life filled with physical, mental, emotional, and spiritual happiness, and the rest of the world will probably look at her and think she is lucky rather than deserving.

One example of how past lives can affect nonfamily relationships is that of a businessman who happened to receive many readings from Edgar Cayce. In fact, these readings are just phenomenal in what they reveal about the profound effects past-life experiences and emotions have on present relationships.

When Walter Morrison walked into a board meeting, he was walking into a history that reached far beyond his present life. Amid the members of this board were souls who had been his conquerors, his servants, his concubines, his cohorts, and his bitter enemies! Imagine what the underlying motivations were when Walter made a proposal on which the group had to vote. And what happened to Walter when he had to cast his vote concerning a proposal by one of the other members of this band of souls. Who among the group would support him? Who would thwart his efforts and ideas? And who would he tend to support and resist? Many of these answers are predictable based on their past-life experiences with each other.

Walter himself was curiously amazed at how well the past-life readings predicted his present feelings for various members of the board. Only in a few cases did he find he really didn't have any particular innate reaction to a member. In most cases, the members who consistently rubbed him the wrong way had been on his bad side in past lives, and those who seemed to agree and support him consistently were those who had done so in the past.

When relationships are viewed with a past-life perspective, the dynamics of the behavior, including the attitudes and emotions in a relationship, become more than just current moodiness or general personality traits. There are undercurrents of memory that simply cannot be easily ignored. Before we look into how we can discover our own past lives, let's examine another teaching from the Cayce material, one that gives us an overview of soul life and soul history through many lifetimes.

# 8

## Destiny, Fate, and Karma

IN ORDER TO fully appreciate the secret teachings, we need to understand how the Universal Law of Cause and Effect works. It's easy to say that the experiences in one's life are the result of past activities, but the forces of this law are greater than we may first imagine.

Every action, every thought, every idle word sets up reactions, according to the Universal Law. When one thinks a thought, that thought makes an impression on the Universal Consciousness. Nothing is ever really unknown, lost, or forgotten. Ultimately, everything is done within the Universal Consciousness, and the whole is affected by it.

This isn't easy for us to believe, living in our own little worlds. Secret, private, and alone are active words in our vocabulary. This is due to our current separation in consciousness from the Universal. In the higher realms of consciousness there is no space and therefore no division. Things and people are not separate, but part of a whole. All is actually one. All is within the whole. By increasing the focus on self, we have created the illusion of a self separated from the rest of life, but it just isn't so. Our individual actions and thoughts make an impact on the Mind of the Universal One.

When the legendary seer, Edgar Cayce, was in the deeper levels of consciousness and was asked to give a "reading" of the soul record for an individual, he found it very difficult to determine whether the soul had *thought* of doing something or had actually *done* it. In the deeper levels of consciousness, thoughts and actions are equal in their impact. Perhaps this explains Jesus' admonition that adultery in one's heart is the same as committing it in deed.

Reactions to past thoughts and actions become our fate, destiny, and karma. An individual's fate is simply the rebounding effects of previous choices remembered by its soul. The reason the effects of these previous choices often seem unfair to the conscious mind is because the *personality* doesn't see beyond its own life for sources of current conditions.

"Master, who did sin, this man, or his parents, that he was born blind?" (John 9:1–2) Now if these disciples didn't believe in and understand preexistence of the soul and karma, why would they ask if this man's own sins had caused him to be *born* blind? The only way this could happen is for him to have sinned *before* his birth! And, in fact, that is just what they thought he might have done. Notice also how the disciples thought that his parents might have brought this upon themselves through past mistakes. Here is a clear indication that within the inner circle of Jesus' followers there was the concept that misfortune had a source, and that that source could extend beyond the present lifetime.

As companions of God, we are free to live and choose

and grow almost as we desire, but not without being subject to Universal, Spiritual Law. Through meeting our thoughts, actions, and words we learn to discern wisdom from folly, lasting strength from weakness, and true life from illusion. In turn we become more able to fulfill our ultimate purpose for existing: to *be* a companion to the Universal Creator. The law is actually a magnificent tool for perfect learning. It is completely impersonal—everyone experiences it equally and for the purpose of enlightenment, even Jesus: "Though he were a Son, yet learned he obedience by the things which he suffered."(Hebrews 5:8)

## The Memory Complex

The law of karma is not some fierce god in the sky keeping track of everything so that it can zap people when they least expect it. Most karmic reactions come from the individual's own deep memory of what he or she has done.

You see, actions and thoughts build a consciousness just as exercise and food build a body. In a way, we are a memory complex. Our body and mind are the sum total of all we have done. The memories, whether conscious or unconscious, make up our present condition. Thus, when we look at one another we are actually seeing a memory complex. Decisions are based on our past; reactions are based on our past; so are our goals. To understand a person, we must know something about his or her memory complex.

Not surprisingly, karma has been described as memory. Karma is memory coming to consciousness again. What has occurred in the past is recalled and has an effect on the present. Now, the recollection may not surface to the conscious level; the personality may have no awareness of the memory, in fact. Yet, it exists at the deeper, soul level. Nevertheless, the soul sees through the same eyes as the personality and is reminded of its past use of free will and consciousness. And so our memory is an important concept in understanding how the law of karma works.

As a soul draws closer to the Universal Mind it becomes aware that some of its memories are not compatible with the Creator, and because its ultimate purpose for existing is companionship with the Creator, it seeks out opportunities to resolve these incompatible memories.

Suppose a soul criticizes another soul among its peers and behind its back. As it becomes more aware of its true nature it will recall this wrong, and because of its incompatibility with the Creator, will seek to correct it. Now, the resolution could take many forms. The soul might seek out an opportunity to work closely with the injured soul as a supporter, assistant, publicist, agent, or the like. Or perhaps it would seek to re-create the original scene—putting itself in a position to criticize the other soul again in front of the same peers. The test would be to see if the soul would choose not to criticize this time, even if it meant a certain loss of position for itself. Throughout all of this the soul grows wiser and more compatible with the Creator.

If, however, a soul has gotten so far away from its true nature that it has no conscience, then the Universal Law can become a formidable obstacle to any further free-will action. Such a soul becomes surrounded by its karma; everywhere it turns it meets the terrible effects of its previous actions and thoughts. Yet, even a soul who has gotten in this pathetic situation can return to perfection because there is *no total condemnation* from the Creator or the Law. If the soul turns away from its self-centeredness and begins acting, reacting, thinking, and speaking like a companion to the Universe, then the Law is just as perfect as it is with error; and the reactions begin to build and establish a new destiny for that soul.

Karma is memory. As one recalls or relives situations, one meets self again, and a new decision point or crossroads is presented to the soul. "Before thee are set good and evil. Choose thou." (Deuteronomy 30:15) In our portrait of life, good would be equated with compatible, harmonious actions and thoughts that consider the needs and desires of others along with those of the self. Evil would be equated with actions and thoughts that are motivated by a self-orientation that pays little or no attention to the needs and desires of others and the whole. Metaphysically speaking, good results in oneness, and evil results in a sense of separation. Decisions in one's life then might better be approached by evaluating which choices promote greater oneness and which promote separation.

However, it gets a little difficult to support this idea much further because in most of the secret teachings there is the belief that one must separate oneself from the world in order to awaken to the greater reality beyond this life. Yet if we look closely at this belief, we can see that it is more accurately a *detachment* than a separation. One is supposed to strive to release oneself from the *possessive power* of the things of this world while still actively participating in it. In other words, one is to enjoy food and drink without being possessed by food and drink; one is to enjoy material life without being possessed by it.

Look at the "Seven Deadly Sins" of Western religion. Each of them (lust, envy, greed, gluttony, etc.) expresses a type of possessive power that overtakes the individual. The "Seven Virtues," on the other hand, express selflessness on the part of the recipient: kindness, gentleness, patience, etc.

Notice also that the sins are mostly self-experienced, but the virtues require another person in order for them to be realized. This follows Jesus' teaching, "I seek mercy, and not sacrifice. He who has ears . . ." Sacrifice can be done alone, but mercy requires that one reach out beyond oneself and consider others and their needs.

Again, we come to the inevitable conclusion that sin is *self* to the exclusion of others and the whole, while virtue is oneness with the whole and consideration of others. It's important to note here that the ultimate goal is not the complete loss of self-identity, but, as Cayce so aptly phrased it: to know yourself to be yourself, yet *one with the whole*.

## Grace, Mercy, and Forgiveness

In one sense it is true that "not one jot or tittle shall be removed from the Law." Each soul must meet every bit of its karma. However, there is a way that it can be modified, softened, even ameliorated. If a soul, knowing another has wronged it, forgives that soul and holds no lingering resentment, it then begins to take hold of the power of forgiveness. The more it forgives, the more it perceives and understands forgiveness. Then, when the soul approaches the Universal Consciousness and realizes it possesses memories that are incompatible with it, forgiveness is much more viable, removing the barrier between Father/Mother and son/daughter.

The law is so precise (what one gives one receives; without exception) that if one begins having mercy on and forgiveness of others, one begins to receive mercy and forgiveness upon oneself. Now, the law is very sensitive to the deep, true purpose for which one does something. If the purpose for forgiving another is simply to obtain forgiveness for oneself, then little is gained. But if one truly forgives by understanding, through empathy and compassion, then there is no way one can avoid receiving forgiveness upon oneself. Unless, of course, one refuses to forgive oneself. Here the law is held captive to the absolute power of free will given to each soul.

The law also works in some very curious ways. Somehow one's greatest weakness has the potential to become one's greatest strength. With each difficult situation, whether physical, mental, or spiritual, there comes an opportunity. These "opportunities" sometimes appear to be hopeless problems, like a crippling disease, an uncontrollable habit, or a situation in which one feels totally victimized without cause. More often they appear as annoyances or frustrations, like an unattractive nose, a difficult sibling, spouse, colleague, boss, lover, or friend or an ever present lack of money. In each case, the soul has an opportunity to resolve and overcome some weakness in itself, and by doing so with the right attitude, the soul can rise to new heights of consciousness, love, and companionship. Attempting to sidestep one's burdens is simply a temporary diversion, delaying the eventual glorification that is the soul's inheritance when it is sought.

And yet, no soul is given more than it can bear to carry—

this is the paradoxical blessing hidden in the limitations of time and space. A soul is given the time it needs to turn away from its selfish ways and, like the prodigal son, return home to a feast of joy and welcome from its Father in heaven. Reincarnation is not a way to avoid judgment and responsibility; it is a way to allow the soul enough time to correct its mistakes and develop itself.

## Fatalism and Free Will

How can free will coexist with fate?

Suppose while traveling on a road you arrive at a point where the road divides into two and you must decide which road you will take. Once you make your decision, you have set a direction that can be almost totally predicted. In this way your fate is decided; but remember, it was your free decision that cast it in the first place.

Now suppose that you could fly up in the air and get a bird's eye view of the road you selected to travel. From this vantage point you would see your future. The catch is that you couldn't be absolutely sure you'd stay on this road once you started. You might decide to go back to the beginning and take the other road, or you might choose to take a side road. You might even decide to sit down for a long time in one place. In this way, your fate is before you, but you still have the free will to change your direction. It may take you some time before you can make a significant change, and perhaps it will require some considerable effort. For example, let's suppose you did decide to travel a different road. Where you are on the present road will in some way determine what options are available to you. There may be only one side road within miles. You might be close enough to the beginning of the road to turn around, or too far down the road for that, in which case you'd have to push on until you could choose another route. Many of the decisions in our lives are like this. They are affected by our original choices, which may be long forgotten by now. The present road we're taking also affects our options. Nevertheless, no matter where we are in our lives, no matter what circumstances in which we find ourselves, once we finally wake up and take notice of what we're doing, our free will is at our disposal to effect the necessary changes. The only limitations are how long it will take us to get to the place where we can make a significant new choice, and how much effort will be required to get there.

## "It's My Karma"

One of the most distorted views of karma is the idea that nothing can be done about it. No matter how terrible our predicament, there is always something we can do, even if it's just dealing with it as best we can with a patient smile, a good attitude, and a loving heart. The time will come when we will be through with this stretch of the hard road, and it's best to come out of it with no bitterness. Remember, no one has done this to us. It is a result of our own actions, thoughts, or words. In patience we will overcome it and rise again to an even greater level than before. Again, let's keep in mind that in the worst situation often lies the greatest opportunity.

## The Center in the Midst of Conditions

From the ancient Taoist text *The Secret of the Golden Flower*, we find another wonderful concept: Amid all the circumstances of our life, all its activities, all its demands and burdens, there lies deep within us an undisturbed, unmoved place of ultimate quiet and peace. This is the center in the midst of conditions. When we learn how to enter this place for short periods each day, the demands of the day lose much of their sting. We find we cannot only cope better, but we can actually make better decisions, necessary changes and effect better use of our time and energy each day. Later, in chapter 11, we'll look at some of the techniques for entering this special place. But now, let's continue our exploration of the role memory plays in the relationship between our past and present lives.

# 9

## Past-Life Memory

THE QUESTION CRYING out for an answer is, "If we have lived before, why don't we remember it?" The answer is both simple and complex.

The simple answer is, "Because we have *not* lived before."

This is not completely true, but it is *relatively* true because the "you" and "I" that we consider to be ourselves have not lived before. We think of ourselves as composed of mind (which includes the personality) and body. The current conscious mind, personality, and body are new; they have *not* been alive before. Nor have they reincarnated in the true sense of the word. However, our *souls* have been alive before—this is the distinction—and they have reincarnated. The memories are thus our souls', not ours.

Now, we might well ask, "If the memories aren't ours, how can they affect us?" It happens much in the same way that a father's memories affect his son. The son does not possess the father's memories, but he'll not easily avoid the influence of them on his own life. If the son wishes to know of the experiences that shaped his father's attitudes, emotions, opinions, beliefs, and personality, and subsequently affected the son, then the son must seek out the father and discover what life has been like for him.

In a similar way, our souls' memories are not consciously our own, but because we are the offspring of our souls, we can't help but be influenced by them. If we are to understand these influences, we must seek out our souls and learn of their experiences. Only then can we completely understand why we are the way we are and consequently why our lives are the way they are.

Now that I've given the simple answer, let's look at the more complex aspects of past-life memory.

## The Path of the Soul

Upon death, the mind and soul are released from the body. Communication with friends and relatives who are still incarnate isn't possible anymore. The soul can't operate the vocal cords of the now dead body to produce sounds that vibrate the ear drums of the incarnate. And the soul can't animate the dead body anymore either. The new, nonphysical "body" does not project into the third dimension, so it can't be seen by three-dimensional beings. Usually, it is this initial inability to communicate and be seen by humans that causes the soul to realize that "death" has occurred. When this realization reaches its ultimate enlightenment, the *conscious* mind begins to relinquish its hold on consciousness, in much the same way that we let go of consciousness as we fall asleep. Thereafter, the *subconscious* mind rises to become the more dominant consciousness, as it does during sleep. In death, the subconscious mind, which is a higher-dimensional mind, will eventually become the operative consciousness for life beyond the three dimensions of Earth.

In order to reincarnate and function again in Earth's dimension, the soul must develop another three-dimensional consciousness. Since this new conscious mind is neither the consciousness used in the realms beyond physical life nor the conscious mind used in the former incarnation, it does not possess of itself any memories of previous lives. Such memories are stored deep within the subconscious, the *soul's* mind.

At or near the time of death, the strongest influence during the most recent incarnation will become prominent, much in the same way that the strongest influences of an Earth day affect the dreams of night. This influence will act as an impelling force upon the soul. As the soul takes stock of the life, it will be moved by this force and seek or be driven toward its next environment—ever reaching for or being forced to accept the environment it has earned.

How all of this occurs depends on the level of spiritual awareness possessed by the dying individual. In cases where there is little or no awareness, the forces of direction are involuntary, ruled by the Law of Cause and Effect. However, where there is some awareness of spiritual purpose and reality, the soul can use its free will during this transition to move toward a dimension of life of its own choosing.

In whatever environ it seeks or finds itself, the soul may sojourn for anywhere from a few years to many thousands of years before it returns to Earth. In many cases, Edgar Cayce found that the length of time the soul remained away from Earth was pertinent to present-life issues.

An example of a short period between incarnations is that of a little girl who was killed during the bombing of England in World War II. She reincarnated within a year of her death. Because she had an uncontrollable fear of loud noises, her mother came to Edgar Cayce for help. The reading revealed that the child's soul had not completely withdrawn from the Earth's environs after that life, causing memories of the bombings to be very near the surface consciousness. Consequently, when she heard loud noises, her subconscious would bring forth images, smells, and sounds, causing her to actually reexperience the bombings with all the emotions of the original moment. She would relive the separation from the mother, the confusion, and the accompanying anxiety. No amount of reassurance that these were just fantasies was going to help the child. They were not fantasies to her. She really experienced these things.

Cayce's advice was to reassure the child that this was a new life, a new opportunity. (This approach would be acceptable to her subconscious mind, but telling her that they were unjustified fantasies would not.) And be sure, he advised protectively, that scary stories and the like are not introduced to her.

Cayce also gave readings which stated that many of the souls reincarnating toward the end of the twentieth century and the beginning of the twenty-first, were ancient Atlantians who had not reincarnated since Atlantis! According to Cayce's own timetable, this would mean that these souls had not reincarnated for hundreds of thousands of years. The reason, according to Cayce, was that their technological understanding was so great that there simply wasn't anything on Earth to interest them until the industrial and technological revolutions began.

These souls would be experiencing their new Earth life much differently than the little girl from World War II. After all, they would have had over one hundred thousand years to assimilate and temper the effects of their most recent incarnation. Those souls who had been reincarnating more often might perceive the returning Atlantians as rather awkward people. According to Cayce, they would not have as natural an understanding of Earth life as souls who had been reincarnating frequently. They might not know, for example, to come in out of the rain, or to tie their shoes to avoid tripping, or appreciate the cycles of night and day. They might not have as much understanding of their bodies as we do. In many ways they would be different, and the Earth would be strange to them. On the other hand, they would likely have an unusually high understanding of the forces of the cosmos, such as electricity, physics, relativity, etc.

## The Soul's Memory Clusters

If past-life memories abide in the mind of the soul, it would seem that all one has to do is to get in touch with one's soul and the memories will pour forth. Alas, it's not that easy.

As best as I can determine from years of study, observation, and personal searching, our souls' reality is quite different from our conscious, three-dimensional reality. In the realm of the soul there is no time, no space. Try as we might, it is hard for us to understand a realm in which linear perception of time does not exist, where spacial separation isn't known. In other words, there is no past, no future; no here and no there. The soul apparently perceives life as a whole. Thus, here and there are the same; yesterday and today are one. Because of this, the memories of past lives are not laid out on an easy-to-read linear timetable for us to scan and comprehend. This is not to say that they can't be translated into linear terms so that we can see with our time/space consciousness, but that requires a skill few acquire.

Let me explain this as I have come to understand it. There is evidence that the deeper consciousness stores memories in *clusters* rather than in sequence. These clusters have little relation to the time frame in which they occurred; in other words, they are not identified by time but rather by similarity. For example, memories of grief are clustered together and are not easily separated into a timetable based on when our souls experienced the grief. Therefore, when one attempts to go into the soul's mind and retrieve memories, one may come upon the "grief cluster" and get a collection of scenes from many different occasions related to grief.

I just used the description "scenes related to grief," but when a person actually contacts his or her grief cluster, it is much more *emotional* than this description conveys. I've observed individuals recalling, or more properly, *reliving*, experiences of their souls. I can tell you that even though we don't have a conscious awareness of these memories, they are very, very much a part of us. And when we do contact them, we can expect to be amazed at how powerful they are and how familiar. A natural result of such contact is a catharsis. Often, the outer individual will later say, "I always 'knew' this but could never express it."

The veil between our conscious and our unconscious is so fine that the slightest turn in the mind can make direct contact. And yet, it is so perpendicular to our current world that no amount of conscious effort can make it happen. Nevertheless, when we make contact, despite our present assurances that we have no memory of another part of us and its experiences, we will come to realize that we *knew* even when we said we didn't. It's that subtle, that close.

I observed a woman coming into contact with her grief cluster through a technique called Guided Imagery Music (GIM). I thank God that this occurred in the presence of an experienced, well-trained clinical therapist. (The therapist was Carol Bush, the author of a soon-to-be published book, *Imagery Through Music: A Way of Knowing*.) The power of this patient's grief was more than I could have dealt with myself. Her body writhed with her soul's sorrow and pain when it contacted the grief. An emotional force rose out of her unconscious to a level greater than I had ever witnessed. However, after several therapy sessions, she was a new woman! Happy, hopeful, and somehow released from the grief that had possessed her soul.

As for this woman's past lives, the GIM method revealed seemingly disconnected scenes of terrible destruction and death. The images that came forth were of towns and roadsides after what seemed to have been battles or wars. After these battles, the women who survived had to live among the dead, struggling to rebuild their lives with nothing. Bodies were everywhere; mostly, she recalled, children's bodies. Sometimes the scenes she described were so sorrowful, so pitiful that I couldn't bear to hear any more. Yet, today I look around the world and see women in similar scenes of terrible destruction and death—Lebanon, Ethiopia, Cambodia, Armenia, and on and on. At some point in their souls' journey, these women will also need to be healed of their grief.

## Patterns of Soul Memory

In addition to the clustering characteristic, soul memories often reflect their presence through *recurring* situations and patterns of behavior in our lives. They are, in fact, the surface signs of subtle soul memory in action. All of us have noticed ourselves' or others' struggle with recurring tendencies to attract certain situations or people in our lives. "He was always attracted to losers." Or, "She never could handle disappointments." "He never believed he was good enough, or smart enough, or rich enough, etc."

If we find ourselves experiencing a certain situation or behavior again and again, you can bet we are seeing the effects of past activities involving the same type of situation or behavior. And the best thing we can do about it is face it in this life and make it right. If we have a weakness for something, we must strengthen ourselves. If we have barriers in our lives, we must patiently but consistently surmount them.

Let me give you another example from the Cayce readings. Edgar Cayce himself had a strong tendency to sink into deep, dark depressions when things began to go wrong in his life—more than would be considered normal for any of us. When he received one of his own readings on this tendency, he was told that it was the result of an action he chose in a past life in ancient Troy. He had been one of the guards at the gates of Troy when the Greeks brought the gift of the towering horse. When the Trojans realized that they had been tricked, and subsequently lost their city and the war because of it, Cayce couldn't bear it and took his own life. As a result of this past decision, he had to fight to keep himself from taking a similar course whenever things went bad for him. The reading went on to say that with every disappointment in this life, he had the opportunity to change the course of events, to find a new way of dealing with failure—a way that required more strength and purpose than his previous choice. Not surprisingly, he learned this lesson well and became quite patient with disappointments and setbacks, learning to endure beyond them to future successes.

For our purposes here, we need to see this as a recurring behavioral pattern in his life: whenever things went wrong he fell apart. Now, those around him at the time probably said to one another, as we might have, "Why does he take it so hard?" "Can't he handle the heat?" They may even have thought of him as "immature." The truth was that deep in his unconscious lay a memory of a failure and the resulting choice he had made. The pattern was set. Every future failure would "remind" him of this great failure, and he would begin again to think of himself as worthless and not deserving of life and another chance.

Remember the woman with so much grief in my previous story on GIM? Her personality and life displayed patterns related to her past-life experiences. She had an unusually emotional sensitivity to children. She couldn't stand any form of violence, especially where children were concerned. Though she adored children and desired intensely to have her own, she was afraid to have them for fear of losing them. These were all patterns of behavior stemming from her soul's experience with death and war.

Other souls who have not had the experiences that Cayce and this woman had would in all probability not find these patterns in their own lives. On the surface, they might not understand why Cayce and the woman reacted to life the way they did, or why certain situations had such an impact on them.

Recurring patterns of behavior are surface signs of past-life experiences and decisions, as are situations in which we find ourselves again and again. Keep an eye open for them, for they are part of your soul's karma and need to be dealt with and healed. As some have described them, they are signs of "unfinished business."

## Techniques for Recalling Past-Life Memories

It is possible to access the soul's perspective and to translate it into a time/space reality in order to learn about ourselves. For Edgar Cayce, the time/space setting was a "book." His deeper self perceived another soul's story as written in the "book of life," and his soul traveled to a Hall of Records where the Book of Life of each soul was stored. When looking at a soul's record, he turned the pages of the book to the left and perceived that he was moving through time into the soul's past; flipping pages to the right, he looked into their future. The book was a translating tool. However, when pressed on the issue, Cayce's deeper consciousness would respond to the question of time and space as not existing in the higher dimensions.

But, for our purposes, we need the translation into time/space reality. Some of the major techniques for making contact with our past-life memories are: hypnotic age-regression, reverie, guided imagery, bodywork, psychic readings, and self-realization. We'll explore each of these methods and you may want to further investigate them yourself in order to find the one that works best for you.

## Regression, Reverie, Guided Imagery

Regression, reverie, guided imagery, and various forms of bodywork all begin by getting the conscious, waking self into a passive, relaxed condition. This allows us access to the deeper consciousness; or, some might say that it is allowing the deeper consciousness to come closer to the surface. However we look at it, these techniques seek to subdue the normal outer self and access the inner self.

Reverie, guided imagery, and bodywork don't set up a time/space reality as clearly as hypnotic regression. In regression the outer self is given a time reality or time frame to work within. The subject begins going back along the time continuum of his or her current life until the moment of birth. At this point the suggestion is given by the facilitator to continue beyond and describe scenes that occurred before birth. This is actually how some of the traditional psychotherapists stumbled unknowingly into the very real realm of past-life memory.

In reverie and guided imagery, the conscious self is simply encouraged to view images from the subconscious, with the expectation that whatever comes up will be of importance to the soul. Or the conscious self can be guided to images related to a specific issue. Past-life memories are not always the primary focus of reverie, imagery, and bodywork, although "cluster" memories as they relate to present issues (specific relationships, phobias, emotional pain, etc.) usually emerge.

## Knowing What Is Real

Where imagination ends and true past-life recall begins is difficult to say. There is no sure way to know whether the past life is imagined or true. In hypnotic cases, we know that the subconscious is so amenable to suggestion that even the slightest variation in the tone of the hypnotist's voice can lead the subject to respond in a certain way. In reveries and guided-imagery sessions, the conscious mind is encouraged to imagine, making it very difficult to know when one is imagining or having genuine past-life recall.

After observing several sessions with Carol Bush, and experiencing a few of my own, there are some ways that one can tell when something genuine is happening. Carol taught me to watch for a change in the nature of the images being experienced by the subject. There is a noticeable difference between images caused by outer stimuli and those coming out of true contact with the unconscious. It's as though the subject, who for the first part of the session seems in control of their images, loses control. The images begin to drive the outer person rather than the other way around. One also begins to see an *emotional* edge to the images. The outer person becomes affected by the images that it sees, no longer able to observe them objectively. These are signs, according to Carol and other researchers, that genuine areas of reality in the inner person have been contacted. Whether they are actual indications of a previous incarnation of the soul or simply indications that the soul preexisted, though perhaps not incarnate, is very difficult to determine and doesn't really matter. The images are true expression from the unconscious and have great value if for that fact alone.

I suggest that the only way we can be sure they are past-life memories is to be as honest as possible about our reactions to the recall experience. If there is simply no identification with the scenario, perhaps it is of no significance. However, I would also suggest that one never completely discard it because it may take time to realize the relevance of the information. It was common for people who received Cayce past-life readings to write years later that they only recently became aware of just how accurate their readings were.

Another way to protect ourselves from excessive or confusing fantasy is to select the hypnotist or guide with great care. If possible, read some of their cases; interview some of their former clients. We need to use *common sense* in choosing both the person and the procedure to which we are subjecting ourselves. Our outer selves seem to have a built-in barrier that protects us from the direct impact of our soul's past experiences, especially those that are harmful or so unpleasant as to ruin any chance of correcting those mistakes in the present. This should be kept in mind when attempting to discover our souls' past. Some of the memories are hidden for a very good reason. Bringing them to the surface by force could prove disastrous, crushing the outer person under a burden that even his or her own soul would not have sanctioned. The past does need to be investigated and awakened, but the outer ego personalities involved in these investigations (e.g., hypnotists, guides, and even the subjects) must not assume they know what's best. The inner soul must be allowed to reveal its secrets in a manner that suits its purposes and timing.

Before leaving these techniques for past-life recall, let's briefly look at body memory.

## Physical Reminders

The physical body may appear to have a distinctly separate reality from that of the soul's, but in *truth*, it is a manifestation of the soul. Therefore the physical body contains within it the soul's memories. If we create the right atmosphere and perform certain manipulations, the body can connect with these memory "pockets" and release them.

Many times in the Cayce readings people were given past-life or even soul-sensitive reasons for present bodily marks, scars, and mannerisms. Just a few examples would include the eldest son of Edgar Cayce who was told in a reading that a scar that appeared on his hand every time he lost his temper was the soul's memory of losing a thumb in an angry past-life fight during the Crusades. The rage remains within him and manifests itself whenever he begins to lose his temper again. In another reading, a woman was told that the marks on her body (from birth) were given to her by a high priest when she first manifested in a physical body as reminders of her spiritual lineage.

There was also the case of a newborn baby who was jaundiced. When the nurses put him under the special lights to heal the jaundice a tattoo of an anchor appeared. When he was removed from the lights the tattoo was not visible! Perhaps the memories are right under our skin.

There are various techniques for releasing body memory. Most of the ones I've learned begin with relaxing the body and mind, carrying it away with music, smells, lights, or other stimuli, then massaging or pressing certain points on the body. Usually the practitioners are looking for the tell-tale signs that give away the location of a memory—*emotion!* When an emotional reaction to touching a certain place on the body occurs, the practitioner begins to ''work'' that area. As this is done, the participant begins to experience feelings, images, smells, or sounds. There may only be an emotional feeling, such as grief, joy, love, etc., without any clear storyline, or there may be a most detailed story accompanying the release. Usually the recall or release begins with fragments, and as the sessions continue, the story and meaning develops.

## Dreams and Self-Realization

Two other sources for past-life recall are dreams and self-realization. Traditionally, these two have been the least appreciated methods, although that attitude is beginning to change. Our dreams and self-realizations have an added bonus in that they not only provide us with past-life information but they do so in a way that builds a closer relationship between our outer and inner selves, integrating the two separate parts of our being. Building this bridge between our two islands of consciousness is vital to eternal life.

Using dreams and self-realization to uncover information about our past lives and the past lives of those around us takes more time than the other methods we've discussed. They also require concentrated and diligent effort on the part of the seeker and so they may be more difficult. But the eventual friendship that can develop from the reintegration of our conscious mind with our subconscious, our body with our spirit, our personality with our soul, is worth all the work involved.

Sleep brings our consciousness to the door of the subconscious. In this way, dreams are the conscious mind's recollection of the subconscious's activities during the deepest phases of sleep. If the conscious level recalls the dream, records it, studies it, discerns a meaning and, finally, *uses* the knowledge in its life, then the parts of the individual begin to reunite and life takes on new dimensions. Since the deeper levels (the subconscious) are not confined to the dimensions of time and space, the past, even the distant past, is not difficult to know. It is here that the soul's story can be found. The following dream is an example of how a past life can be discovered through dreams.

> I woke up around two or three in the morning thinking someone had made a loud noise in my bedroom. As I looked around I saw that everything was quiet. Nothing had happened. Lying back on my pillow I began to recall what I had been dreaming just before waking. The strong smell of horses, leather, and sweat was overwhelming. It was as though these things were right in my bedroom. In my mind's eye

I saw the side of a horse and a portion of a leather saddle. I couldn't have been more than a few inches from them. My vision was strange. It was as though I were looking through a pipe. I only saw what was directly in front of me, no peripheral vision at all. Slowly I started to look down at what I suppose was my feet. I was wearing black boots which were covered with a dry film of dirt. The ground around my feet was dusty dirt with little patches of scrub grass. I stared at my boots and the dirt for a long time. I began to feel how sweaty my feet were inside these boots and I didn't like it. Suddenly I heard someone behind me. He was calling me, but he was calling me "Lexington." Somehow I knew this was my name in this place so I turned around to see who was calling. As I looked at the man I knew he was my brother, Tim. He didn't look like Tim but I knew it was he. He told me to come over where he was and get something to eat before we rode on. It was as though I was drugged. It was very hard to walk but I managed to move over toward him and some other men sitting around a campfire. Like a slow-motion camera, my eyes took in everything though I didn't know what was going on. As I sat down to eat I began to smell the fire and the food. I still could smell horses, leather, and sweat. The smoke of the fire was strong and somehow familiar. I looked over at Tim and wondered if he'd noticed that I wasn't really Lexington. But he just looked up at me and told me to hurry up and eat, it wasn't safe for us to linger around here too long. Since I couldn't see except for what was directly in front of me, I began to worry that I wouldn't be able to find the food and eat. Somehow my hands found the food and I slowly ate. Then suddenly I realized that this was a past life, that I had actually lived this life with my present brother Tim. During this realization I had the feeling my mother in that life was behind me and I turned to see her. She introduced me to some of her friends. I was afraid she was going to ask me to tell them my name but I didn't know it. However, she turned to her friends

and said, "This is my son, Lexington." I was dumb-
founded. I just looked at her, dressed in the clothes of
an American settler, and wondered what this was all
about. Then just as suddenly I saw a map of North
America. A dark, bold line began to move across the
map and I knew it was showing me where I had
traveled during this lifetime. When the line stopped
moving I knew that was where I died and I became
uncomfortable because the death experience began
coming back to me. The scene was once again around
the campfire with my brother and the other men. Tim
looked up at me and I knew he loved me. He also
knew what was about to happen and his heart was sad
because he didn't want me to die. I heard a rustling
noise in the bushes to my left side but since my vision
could only see directly in front of me I couldn't see
who was coming. I felt a powerful blow to my head
and as I started to lose consciousness I looked over at
Tim who was shooting his gun as fast as he could and
yelling, "No, No! Don't die, Lex! Don't die!"
Somehow I knew we'd be together again but it was
over for now. Nothing could be done to keep me
alive. My face was lying in the dusty dirt and I just
stayed there, looking at the dirt, feeling my breath
move in and out of my nostrils. I felt sorry for Tim.
I didn't want him to be left without me and I didn't
want him to be so sad. Somehow I felt I had always
been a burden to him. I was never tough enough or
smart enough for this wild, untamed country. I
thought to myself, "I'll make this up to him. I'll
make sure the next time we're together I stay with
him through the entire life, never leaving him." Then
I heard a whirring sound in my ears and I knew I was
leaving this life. It was this noise that woke me.

In the present life this dreamer had a younger brother
called Tim, and he was very protective of him. The two of
them went everywhere together. However, the man who
had this dream was getting married in a week and was

planning to move away from his younger brother to live in his wife's hometown. But the dream affected him so much that he asked his younger brother to transfer to a college in his wife's hometown. Tim did just that and the two of them continue to be very close.

Most past-life dreams aren't so complete and detailed, revealing only fragments of a past life. Usually the fragment is an image, smell, or sound that has left a lasting impression on the soul's mind. For example, a college professor frequently awoke from a nightmare in which he was choking on sand. The dreams were so real that he would actually be choking when he awoke. This professor was a white man who specialized in Black Studies. He had always found black culture and history to be of great interest to him. One day he was listening to a lecture by Alex Haley in which Mr. Haley told of how Africans kidnapped by the slave traders, bound and left on the beaches waiting to board slave ships, would commit suicide by deliberately swallowing sand. The professor was stunned. He knew immediately what his dream was about. He was recalling the most powerful image in his mind as he had committed suicide on the beaches of Africa in a previous life. A traumatic death experience from a past life is often recalled because of the profound impression it leaves on the soul's mind. Such was the case with this professor, the image and sensation staying with him in the form of a recurring dream.

Again, the only way we can distinguish between a true life recall and an imagined one is to objectively see how well it fits with our present character and life. In the case of the professor, his present interests and career supported the dream and the subsequent realization that he had lived a past life as a black African man who had committed suicide by swallowing sand.

Here's another example. The dreamer had this dream three days before he was to marry. He had been feeling anxious about the marriage because his bride-to-be did not have the same enthusiasm for the marriage as he did. Here's the dream he received.

> Dreamed I was dressed in old Spanish clothing and did not look as I do today. In the dream I had dark hair and a beard. I was standing in a long rowboat that was slowly heading to shore. Somehow I knew we were off the coast of what is now called St. Augustine, Florida, but then it was wilderness. As we moved slowly toward shore I looked back at the ship that brought us here. It was surprisingly small for crossing the Atlantic Ocean; all wood and ropes and canvas. On the deck I saw Mary (my wife in the present incarnation), but she didn't look anything like she does today. She had black hair, dark skin and dark eyes, but somehow I knew it was Mary. She held a small baby in her arms. As I watched them a strange image appeared over her shoulder. It was difficult to get this image in focus; I had to strain to see it. But as I looked very closely and intently, it began to take shape, and to my astonishment, it was my face as it is today! It was me, not as I was in the dream but as I look now—looking over her shoulder back at me! Suddenly I knew what the vision meant. I was about to die and I would not be able to care for Mary and the baby, but *he*, my future self, would care for them in another life. I continued to stare at his face as if to get absolute assurance that Mary, the baby, and I would have another chance. Glancing back at Mary and my baby, I began feeling very sad that they would have to continue life in this rough land without me to help them. As I looked back at his face I kept holding fast to the idea that he would be able to care for them in the future and give them

much of the joy they were going to miss in this lifetime. Then I turned away and looked at the shore-
line. It was heavily wooded and desolate. There was
no sign of trouble. Then, without warning, the beach
was filled with savages. They were wild, crazy people, yelling and screaming with a violent madness
that was terrifying. I watched the whole thing develop with a deep sense of my unavoidable destiny.
I felt a piercing pain in my chest, penetrating the life
inside me. As I fell into the water, I turned again to
the ship and saw my wife and child on the deck,
motionless, with the future face looking back at me
over her shoulders. There was no expression on their
faces, and as I slowly sank in the water I continued
staring at them with all the feelings of the tragedy of
the situation and what she and the child were going to
have to go through without me to help.

Little wonder that his bride-to-be was not as enthusiastic
about marrying him; she'd been with him before and it
wasn't anything to hang her hopes on! This dream helped
this young man. Not only did it give him an insight into one
of his previous lives and its effect in his present life, but it
gave him a clear view of a major purpose in this present
incarnation. The opportunity to care for these two souls for
whom he felt so much unfulfilled obligation was one that he
had longed for.

Dreams are an excellent way to get in touch with our
soul's memories, especially because the dream is actually
the soul sharing an experience with the current personality.

## Self-Realization

I'm using the term self-realization as a catchall for intu-
itive perceptions, déjà vu, spontaneous revelation, repeti-

tive mental images, "gut feelings," and all the other forms
of personal insight into our deeper memories. If we open up
to the possibility of reincarnation, we will begin to see
many hints of our souls' past. Our natural talents, our taste
in food, clothing, and stories, our innate characteristics, our
primary interests all indicate our souls' past experiences.
Here's an example.

A young man was working at a printing and mailing
company as a zip code sorter. It's a very nonmechanical
job, requiring that one simply sort the mail by zip code. One
Friday afternoon two of the printing press operators quit
their jobs, leaving the company in a terrible bind. The zip
code sorter asked the manager if he could come in the next
day and work with one of the remaining printers to learn
how to operate the presses. This was a ridiculous request
because printing required a great deal of technical training
and a lengthy apprenticeship before someone could correctly operate a press. But because the circumstances were
so unusual, the manager gave him permission to try. The
young man quickly became one of the best printers the
company had. He said that it was all very natural for him.
The smell of the ink was so familiar to him that he felt good
being around it. He so quickly understood the machines that
he felt he had operated them before. And the process of
printing was easily grasped. He went on to become the
supervisor and eventually the manager of the printing op-
eration.

On a visit to Williamsburg, Virginia, this young man
happened to walk into the old colonial printer's shop that
had been restored to its original condition. Without any
warning, he began to feel very strange. The smell of the

wood, the ink, and the sounds of the wooden press came rushing at him with such intensity he had to leave the building. After sitting outside for several minutes, he got up and went back inside the restored print shop. Slowly he walked through it, somehow knowing that he had worked there in Colonial America. He observed how the costumed tour guides dressed and what they said about different items in the shop, and a deep sense of life's true breadth came upon him. He was never quite the same again. He had gained a new sense of the continuity of life and gained it in a very personal way. It was no longer an intellectual concept for him; he knew it firsthand.

## Psychic Readings

Now you would think that anyone who studied and learned so much from the psychic readings of Edgar Cayce would be a strong supporter of psychic readings for past-life memory. But I'm not. As the popularity of readings of all kinds has soared, there has also been a rise in the number of fakes and charlatans who will say anything for a buck. If you decide to pursue past-life readings, I advise you to do so with caution.

As we have seen with other methods, when we connect with truth it resonates within us and sometimes we find validation for it in our present reality. I have found that the techniques that use the soul to tell the soul's story are the most reliable. In other words, you are your own best source of information. Even Edgar Cayce recommended that we seek within ourselves for the answers and avoid outside sources. However, I do believe some people are sensitive enough to "read" the Akashic Records or the "Book of Life" as Cayce referred to them, giving us some helpful insights into our past and its effects on the present. But you'll have to judge the results with care and common sense.

I recommend you seek within yourself. In the long run it will yield more than memories.

# 10

## The Power of an Ideal

FOR US TO become companions to our Creator some changes are needed. As we have seen, our present condition is not nearly adequate for companioning with the Universal One. But before we change, we need to have some idea of what we're supposed to change into. We need to know the true nature of a companion to the consciousness of the universe.

Now, before we blow our minds on this awesome thought or go running off to live in caves, let's hold to the guideline that the way is achieved step by step, a little here and a little there, and begins with what we presently have at hand. Even though the goal *seems* far beyond us, it isn't. Within us and our present circumstances exist the necessary tools for the necessary transformation. Remember, the caterpillar shows no outward signs of its potential to become a butterfly, and we are much greater than a caterpillar.

## From Flesh to Spirit

First, we need a concept of what a companion is in its perfection. We need an *ideal*, a standard by which we can measure and guide our progress through this metamorphosis. And a metamorphosis it is. We are intending to completely change form, from terrestrial to celestial, from flesh to spirit, from man to god. Has anyone already achieved this? Is there someone we can look to as an example? If we accept that Jesus became one with the Father, transfigured and resurrected his body, then he may well be our best ideal.

When I first got involved with the secret teachings and decided to begin my own transformation, I couldn't accept Jesus as an ideal. Religion, as I experienced it in my early years, destroyed all of that for me. I was subjected to teachers who were convinced that *fear* was the beginning of holiness, and sin was as natural to humans as eating! It took me a long time to get over my terrible bias against anything religious, including the name with which they "beat" me. Perhaps my soul was meeting something it had done to others in the past. Perhaps, in a previous life, I had used Jesus to "club" others into submission, and now I was experiencing the devastating effects of this approach. Whatever, I found it very difficult to accept the Jesus who had been presented to me.

Since then I have come to know at very different Jesus— a loving, humble, meek, and long-suffering Jesus, with a mystical side that I wasn't aware of before. It is this Jesus whom I now believe the secret teachings are talking about. And it is this Jesus whom I suggest we consider as an ideal for the transformation. I don't mean his life as Jesus alone, though this is obviously the primary one to consider, but the complete story of this great soul's experiences. In other words, we must consider his other incarnations and their place in his preparation for the final transformation. It is not within the scope of this book to present all of his lives; I'll leave that to others (see Recommended Reading for such books) or some future book. For now let's focus on the overall ideal to aid our transformation.

## A Living Companion

The Cayce readings make a distinction between Jesus and Christ. Jesus was a human being, like you and me; a man who lived among others in a physical world. He was truly a man in every sense of the word, with weaknesses and strengths common to all. He needed to sleep, eat, love, and be loved. However, this particular man cooperated with the Universal Forces and maintained attunement with the inner presence of God. As he said, he and the Father are one.

Christ, according to Cayce, is the spirit *within* this man. Christ is the light, the wisdom, the eternal aspect within the physical man, Jesus. Here we see again the combining of flesh and spirit, terrestrial and celestial, man and god. It is the way of things in this world. Christ is the spirit; Jesus is the man.

> Truly, truly, I say to you, unless one is born of water and the Spirit, he cannot enter the kingdom of God. That which is born of the flesh is flesh, and that which is born of the Spirit is spirit. (John 3:5–6)

Christ manifested through a human being like ourselves, Jesus of Nazareth; son of Mary and Joseph, brother of James, friend of Lazarus, teacher of Peter and the others. He dined with Zacchaeus, wept with Mary and the others over Lazarus' passing, and asked John to care for his mother as he was dying. The great deeds were not this man's, but the spirit within him. The man made himself a channel, a vessel for the Great Spirit. Thus he transformed himself from a mere human being into a living companion of God.

This is exactly what we want to do. And according to Cayce, "living an ideal" is a most powerful way to effect the desired change. Jesus used a graphic analogy of how he could be used as an ideal, equating himself with the bread of life, spiritual life, as the following Bible passage tells us.

> The Jews then murmured at him, because he said, "I am the bread which came down from heaven." They said, "Is not this Jesus, the son of Joseph, whose father and mother we know? How does he now say, 'I have come down from heaven?' "
>
> Jesus answered them, "Do not murmur among yourselves. No one can come to me unless the Father who sent me draws him; and I will raise him up at the last day. It is written in the prophets, 'And they shall all be taught by God.' Every one who has heard and learned from the Father comes to me. Not that any one has seen the Father except him who is from God; he has seen the Father. Truly, truly, I say to you, he who believes has eternal life. I am the bread of life."
>
> "Your fathers ate the manna in the wilderness, and they died. This is the bread which comes down from heaven, that a man may eat of it and not die. I am the living bread which came down from heaven; if any one eats of this bread, he will live for ever; and the bread which I shall give for the life of the world is my flesh."

The Jews then disputed among themselves, saying, "How can this man give us his flesh to eat?" So Jesus said to them, "Truly, truly, I say to you, unless you eat the flesh of the Son of man and drink his blood, you have no life in you; he who eats my flesh and drinks my blood has eternal life, and I will raise him up at the last day. For my flesh is food indeed, and my blood is drink indeed. He who eats my flesh and drinks my blood abides in me, and I in him. As the living Father sent me, and I live because of the Father, so he who eats me will live because of me. This is the bread which came down from heaven, not such as the fathers ate and died; he who eats this bread will live for ever." This he said in the synagogue, as he taught at Capernaum.

Many of his disciples, when they heard it, said, "This is a hard saying; who can listen to it?" But Jesus, knowing in himself that his disciples murmured at it, said to them, "Do you take offense at this? Then what if you were to see the Son of man ascending where he was before? It is the spirit that gives life, the flesh is of no avail; the words that I have spoken to you are spirit and life. But there are some of you that do not believe." . . . And he said, "This is why I told you that no one can come to me unless it is granted him by the Father."

After this many of his disciples drew back and no longer went about with him. Jesus said to the twelve, "Will you also go away?" Simon Peter answered him, "Lord, to whom shall we go? You have the words of eternal life; and we have believed, and have come to know, that you are the Holy One of God." (John 6:41–69)

It's important to realize that the Jews were correct, they did know his father and mother, and they had probably watched him grow up. From all *outward* appearances this was just a man like other men, and they *knew* this man. How could he have come down from heaven and become the "bread of life?" How could he give them his flesh to eat? From all outward signs this was crazy. Like most of us, they expected Christ to be an external god, not a spirit within a person!

Jesus explains that only someone who has heard God from within will sense the meaning of his words. Such a soul would know the spirit and could sense its presence in another. Jesus also quotes the passage that states that all of us will be taught by God himself (Isaiah 54:13). Why? Because, unlike outward appearances, we are each, from the lowest to the highest, destined to be direct companions to our Creator. No person is before us; each has his or her own *birthright* to direct contact with the Creator. God will teach each of us—from within.

## The Ideal at Work

Even though God will teach each of us directly, Jesus is an ideal, and if we assimilate this ideal into our systems, we will be transformed. It's like saying, I wanted so much to be a dancer that I ate, drank, and slept dancing! Or, as I once heard a famous musical star say, ''I imitated my idols to the point that I knew exactly how they would play anything. I became them. Later, as I started to express music as I felt it, I developed my own style. But it was my complete absorption into the music of my idols that helped me develop to a level at which I could express music as I felt it.'' This is the power of an ideal at work.

Jesus, the embodiment of God in man, was to be eaten, digested, and assimilated as one would do a loaf of bread. In this way the partaker would come to know the true nature of a companion who was one with God, yet living among men in the physical world. Flesh and spirit would be reconciled. Divine and human would be compatible. Finite would rise again to an awareness and companionship with the infinite. Life would become continuous; death and separation a thing of the past.

There are two important parts of this concept to keep in mind. First, *God will teach us directly*, from within. We are not out here alone if we are connected within. Secondly, as we study and apply the elements of our ideal, we begin to assimilate it into our systems (body, mind, heart, and soul). This assimilation leads to a transformation that reconciles our contradictions of flesh and spirit, human and divine. God begins to abide with us and we companion with him. One of the tools that can help with the necessary assimilation is meditation. In the following chapter we'll see how it works and how you can learn to use it in your own life.

# 11

## Meditation: Tool for Transformation

DEVELOPING THE ABILITY to enter into deep meditation is a vital step toward achieving higher states of spiritual consciousness and reuniting with our source. Through meditation, a quiet body, a clear mind, and an enlivened spirit can rise to the highest state of being that we can perceive, even into the presence of God. Over a period of time, meditation can help transform us from mere mortal terrestrial beings to immortal, divine companions with the whole. It can help make our present life on Earth a veritable school for soul growth. Everything can have new meaning.

### Free the Mind and Heart

Having the right heart is the first step toward experiencing meaningful, effective meditation. The best techniques won't lift a selfish heart into the presence of the Great Spirit. We must free our minds and hearts from things that distract or interfere with our progress. The right thoughts and actions, the right attitudes and emotions *throughout the day* will do more for our meditation than anything else.

No matter how well we practice meditation techniques, if we don't hold fast to the right heart and mind, nothing will work. It is the pure in heart that see God (Matt. 5:8), not those who are skilled in meditative techniques. Here is an appropriate quote from *The Secret of the Golden Flower:*

> He who lacks the right
> virtue may well find
> something in it, but heaven
> will not grant him his Tao.
> Why not? The right virtue
> belongs to the Tao as does
> one wing of a bird to the other:
> if one is lacking, the other
> is of no use.

Raising the spiritual forces of our bodies and minds should be done for the right reason and should be supported by daily actions and thoughts that reflect this purpose. After meditation, it is vital that we apply ourselves to living the ideal throughout daily life. It does not matter what type of work we do during the day, only that our attitude and purpose support that which we are seeking when we enter meditation. A person can be an inner-city police officer dealing with violence and crime all day and still be able to attune himself to his higher self and the Creator if his actions and thoughts are in accord with his ideal.

## A Meditation Technique

There are many different ways to meditate, but here we will focus on a technique that helps regain spiritual consciousness and union.

Meditation is the quieting of the physical body and conscious mind. When we meditate we are clearing away thoughts and cares of the day. We are attuning to our inner self and from there abiding in a heightened state of awareness and expectancy—listening and waiting for that response from our higher self and the One Spirit. The response comes in many forms, and I don't want to limit its possibilities for you. However, I would like to share what others and myself have experienced.

There are specific techniques and exercises for quieting the body and the mind and arousing our soul. All of them use special *activity* to achieve *inactivity*. Since we each have a different perspective, different experiences, and are at various levels of development, it's best that we each modify the meditation techniques to suit our own comfort and preference. No one method works for absolutely everybody in exactly the same way. The following meditation process is generally very good. It contains some excellent techniques and can be easily modified to suit your personal needs.

## That Special Place and Time

Choose a specific place and time to meditate. This helps develop a pattern of response and readiness within the body for meditation. Regular periods of meditation will accomplish much more than occasional ones. So, select a regular time every day and try not to miss it. In the beginning set aside fifteen minutes each day for meditation. Later you may want an hour.

Cayce often recommended meditating between two and

four in the morning. Many great seekers have used this same period for their private awakening and attunement. Cayce said that it is best if you have already slept for a while before meditating at this time. In this way your body will have had some deep rest and your soul will have had time to awaken to the "nightly wisdom." However, it can be very disruptive to a marriage and a young family! Therefore, keep in mind that the best meditation time is the one you can use regularly. Don't set up two A.M. as your meditation time if you can't stick to it, or it creates so much turmoil that it becomes a stumbling block rather than a stepping stone! I've had good meditations at seven A.M., too.

The important things are a special place and regular time. After you've practiced for some years, you can be more flexible about these requirements, but in the beginning they're very helpful.

## Preparation

Begin by cleansing the body with water. Depending on the circumstances, this can be no more than splashing a little water on your face and washing your hands. Then sit or lie in a comfortable position. If you like, you can use one of the Eastern yoga asanas (positions), but I wouldn't suggest forcing yourself into a position that is so unnatural or uncomfortable as to distract you from achieving *stillness*.

Many people find that doing some stretching exercises before settling down makes the body more relaxed and ready for being in one position for a long time. I use simple stretches of the spine, limbs, and neck. The Edgar Cayce "head and neck exercise" is excellent. Here's how it goes. While standing straight with your arms relaxed at your sides, move the head forward, touching the chest with the chin three times. Then stretch the head backward three times, and then to the left three times and the right three times. Then, circle the head to the left three times, and to the right three times. This not only loosens up the neck and shoulder muscles where a lot of tension forms, but it increases the flow of blood to the head and brain.

Once the preliminary exercises are complete, assume whatever position you have chosen and become still.

## The Breath

Once you are in position, use the Cayce breathing technique to raise the energies of the body. Press your left nostril closed and breathe in through the right nostril, exhaling through the mouth three times. While you are breathing in, think "strength!" Then press the right nostril closed and breathe in through the left nostril, exhaling through the right nostril three times. While you do this, think of quietly awakening your inner spirit.

Don't take breathing exercises lightly. Remember how we became physical beings: "The Lord God breathed the breath of life in him and he became a living soul." Breath is life in this dimension and these exercises use that force to raise the level of our life energy and arouse a response from our inner being. If you can, let this air be fresh. Often the air in closed rooms is very stale, with little oxygen and many unwanted gases. Open a window if you can.

## An Incantation

After you have gotten into position and completed the breathing technique, begin to carry yourself deeper by using an incantation or soft music. Personally, I've found an incantation to be very effective. The sound of your own voice calling forth the spirit within has a lot of power.

Incantate the sound "Oooommmm" (rhymes with "home") while feeling the sound rise from your lower spiritual centers to the higher ones. (Refer to the illustration on p. 39 if you don't remember the location of the spiritual centers.) This sound is universally effective. On the surface it may appear to be an ancient Sanskrit word of little significance, but it is actually a root sound of much power and purpose. There are many other chants that can be used with good results, but "Om" touches a special chord within.

A variation on the Om incantation is "Aaaarrrr-eeeeooooommmm." Here the "aaaa" sounds begin in the lower centers and as the sound changes, the energy rises through the centers to the final sound of "mmmm" at the third eye center.

The secret to successful incantation is to think of it as *inner sounding*. It's not external, like singing. The sounds are meant to *resonate* inside the body cavities, vibrating the spiritual centers and awakening them to a new level.

## The Movement of Energy

At this stage in the meditation, you may begin a technique called "the Circulation of the Light." It is described in detail in the wonderful book *The Secret of the Golden Flower*. The circulation of the light combines the cycle of breathing in and out with the rising and falling of the energy along the path from the lower centers to the higher. In other words, from the gonads up the spine to the pituitary body in the center of the brain system and behind the middle of the forehead. As one breathes in, the abdomen is *drawn in* and the energy rises upward along the spinal cord over the top of the head and down into the chambers of the seventh center. Here it meets with the Universal Creative Forces and is transformed into "living water" (Rev. 22:17). As one exhales it flows down the spinal cord, bathing the centers as it goes. The cycle is continued until you feel a definite raising of the vibrations in the body.

During the circulation along this path and through the centers, the body may become conscious of distinct vibrations. This is different with each individual, but there are some common sensations. One is a sense of *movement* within the body. This can result in a feeling that the body is moving back and forth, side to side, in a circular motion, or levitating. It can culminate at the head or reach to areas above the head, like the flame over the disciples' heads when the Holy Spirit was upon them. Don't go looking for this, let it come naturally. And if it never occurs for you, fine, experience the awakening the way it happens for you. Don't let my words or anyone else's get in the way of *your* potential.

There may also be feelings of lightness, dizziness, and the head being drawn back. Within the spiritual centers one may feel vibrations or pressures. These are indications of an awakening spirit.

## The Ideal

After the circulation of the light has been through enough cycles to raise us to a higher vibrational state, like changing water to steam, we should then move our attention away from the technique and let it go on its own again. Our mind should bring forth the highest ideal we can conceive and focus on the *essence* of that ideal, calling all parts of our being to awaken to it. For example, I bring forth the patience, love, and quiet devotion found in the essence of Christ's life, rather than the specific teachings or actions of his life.

When this ideal is in accord with our superconscious, there may come a flow from "above" to fulfill all that is needed by our minds and our bodies. We may feel stronger, more at one with ourselves and the Universe, and a feeling of peace may come over us. Don't try to possess it. Remain still and silent, in a state of heightened awareness and expectancy, allowing yourself to receive the spirit without conditions.

Now that I've said this, let me "counter" it. Opening yourself up to the inner forces requires discernment. Within the spiritual (inner) dimensions are good *and* evil forces. The Creator has not chosen to destroy the evil ones in hope

that they may choose light and goodness eventually. Therefore, you must protect yourself from the *free-willed* disin-
carnates in the spirit (inner) realms. The tares are still
among the wheat. Therefore, surround your body and mind
with the protection found in the thought of the Light of
Christ, and then discern the spirit to which you attune yourself, and only then open yourself up to the spirit, as a child
would to its mother. Remember, when we seek goodness
with the right heart and mind, we will find it. We must be
as guileless as doves and as cunning as serpents to survive.
I would add that not only do we need to be wary of disin-
carnates, but more often things within our own deep unconscious selves. For within us may be forces of memory and
desire that are too powerful for us to handle. Attune yourself to the spirit; avoid anything less—even though it may
appear in sheep's clothing. This is not intended to frighten
but to warn and prepare you. Meditation is not dangerous if
it is done with proper care and concern, just as driving steel
cars next to each other at sixty-five miles an hour is not
dangerous when done properly.

## The Deeper Realms

It is difficult to define the deeper realms of meditation.
First of all, there just aren't words to describe them. It's as
if they belong to another dimension altogether and will
never be completely describable in three-dimensional terms
and concepts. Secondly, I'm not sure we each experience
these realms in the same way. It's like trying to discover if
we all see the same shade of a color—we may say we do,

but do we ever really know unless we each see it through the other's eyes?

I've never met anyone who experienced the deeper realms every time he or she meditated. So we shouldn't get too caught up in judging our experiences. Sometimes they'll be great and other times just so-so—at least it may appear that way from the outside. And, occasionally, a meditation will be more than we ever imagined, and we'll go in the strength of that meditation for a very long time!

Very few of us can begin meditating and immediately experience the wonders of it all at once. It is best to begin where you are and waste no time wondering why you aren't experiencing this or that. If you "keep on keeping on," then you're bound to experience all of it.

It is easy to become so involved with the techniques and sensations of meditation that we forget to enter the most vital phase: silence. For many of us silence means empti- ness or nothingness; to sit in silence would appear to have little value to it. However, the silence of deep meditation is anything but empty nothingness. It's remarkably revitaliz- ing and rejuvenating; occasionally it's filled with profound sensations, awarenesses, and insights, some of which make such an impression on us that we are changed forever.

Therefore, after you have used the techniques to raise your body's vibrations and your consciousness, and aroused your soul from its slumber, become as still and silent as you can. These moments in deep silence will become some of the most valuable in your life.

> And when he had opened
> the seventh seal, there was

silence in heaven about the
space of half an hour.

                                    Revelation 8:1

## Some Tips

It isn't a good idea to meditate on a full or hungry stomach; it's bad for the digestion and makes it difficult to achieve a deep meditation. If noises are distracting, try using the energy of those noises to raise you to a higher place of consciousness instead of becoming angry or bitter with the outside distractions. If you are caring for children, try to do the best you can to find a reasonably regular period for meditating. If you have a nonsupportive spouse, don't flaunt your meditation in front of him or her; try to find a time when he or she won't be affected by your private pursuit. If you are missing the function of one of your endocrine glands because of surgery or malformation, continue to focus on the area where the gland would normally be and you'll get results eventually—remember the centers are spiritual first and physical second; focus on the spiritual. If you find yourself falling asleep during meditation, don't be too concerned about it. Try to maintain a keen sense of quiet awareness for as long as you comfortably can; then let sleep overtake you, but only after you feel you've reached a level of heightened attunement to your ideal. Sleep frees the soul and is a natural response to deep meditation. But we are also trying to reunite spirit and flesh, so the flesh (your outer self) must take part in the attunement.

Many people experience images, sounds, voices, and other stimuli during meditation. These should be a natural response from your higher self *after* you have reached a keen attunement to your ideal, not intrusions into your meditation. Therefore, control your consciousness in the early stages of meditation, relaxing your hold on it only after you have the ideal well in place.

# 12

## Contact Dreams

IN CHAPTER NINE we briefly discussed the value of dreams in revealing past-life memory. But dreams, like meditation, can be used as an everyday tool for simply staying in touch with ourselves and our spiritual nature.

Dreams are one of the best sources for insight, knowledge, and understanding. When the physical body and conscious mind are quiet in sleep, the deeper levels of consciousness can more clearly express themselves. If one learns to remember these expressions and to correctly interpret them, there is no limit to one's knowledge and understanding.

Surprisingly, the Cayce material says that "Nothing occurs in one's life that hasn't been foreshadowed in a dream!"

How can this be? As we have seen, the predominant level of our consciousness is in the realm of time and space, physical reality. But the deeper levels abide in dimensions beyond time and space and can "see" the road that lies ahead. In fact, these levels of consciousness can also see the road that has been traveled, even back to the beginning of the soul's consciousness. If the conscious mind learns how to listen and understand its deeper levels of consciousness, it can come to know the forces affecting its life, how best to handle them, and what opportunities and perils are ahead. However, the deeper consciousness is not concerned with just the profound or grand things. The everyday needs of life—money, relationships, jobs, diet, physical health, etc.—are all dealt with in dreams. Nothing is too mundane or, for that matter, too grand or holy that one cannot get insight about it from a dream.

## Dream Messages

When the conscious mind and body are asleep, the subconscious and superconscious use the images, events, people, and things of daily physical life to create a somewhat three-dimensional story or message containing information that they need to convey to the conscious level. So in order to get the message that the subconscious and superconscious offer us we must pay attention to our dreams. First, of course, we need to remember the dreams we have. It's usually a good idea to keep a journal of them. Many people say that writing them down helps to jog the memory. Having a record of dreams also gives us the opportunity to study them and find meaning and ultimately discover the message that is being conveyed. But *using* the knowledge is the real value. When we do this, then the whole individual begins to grow and fulfill its purpose.

Sometimes the message of a dream is very literal and clear as in this dream.

> Dreamed Betty would call tomorrow and I should
> not be so cool and distant. She will ask me to come
> visit her and I should go despite my feelings to the
> contrary.

Betty did call this dreamer just as the dream had predicted, and the dreamer did visit her.

Often the message of a dream has a bizarre element that
helps focus the attention of the conscious mind on a particularly important part of the message, as in this dream.

> Dreamed I won my preliminary tennis match but
> as I went over to the stands to be congratulated by
> everyone my head fell off, and kept falling off. No
> matter what I did I couldn't keep my head on my
> shoulders. It was very embarrassing. Finally out of
> frustration I asked if anyone wanted to go watch Stan
> play his match. I figured if I could get them to stop
> looking at me I might be able to keep my head on.

By using this bizarre image the subconscious cleverly
warns the conscious self of the potential for losing one's
head over an initial victory and becoming too confident and
perhaps losing a future match. It even gives him the solution: "Go watch your future opponent play his preliminary
match."

In some cases the message of a dream is strongly stated
in symbols that deeply affect the conscious self, as in this
dream.

> I was in the bowels of an old, gray inner city and
> on the corner was a fast-food restaurant called,
> "Colonel Coffee's Coffins!" When I awoke I did not
> like the feeling of this dream. It was ominous, and I
> felt like it was serious.

The dreamer's excessive use of coffee to keep him going was causing serious problems with his system, perhaps literally in his bowels. This dream could be interpreted on another level as well. It could pertain to his overall life-style of going so fast that he would soon become like a city that had spent its wealth and was decaying.

Interpreting a heavily symbolic dream requires that the dreamer identify what those symbols mean to him. The same symbol from two different dreamers can mean two different things. However, there are universal symbols, but even these should be applied individually. When interpreting one's dreams, be careful not to prejudice your interpretation by looking for what *you want*, or by being *afraid to find* what you hoped for! Be as objective as you can. Pray about the dream. Sometimes it helps to set the dream aside for a while and return to it later with a second viewing.

## Deeper Meanings

When a dream comes from the superconscious mind, its symbolism and imagery is often like that of a vision. I call these *Contact Dreams* because I feel the dreamer has made contact with his superconscious and the Universal Mind. Here's an example.

> I was aboard a large ship with twelve engines. Ten of the engines were working fine, but the eleventh engine was not assembled, and the twelfth wasn't even there! When I began to assemble the eleventh engine I heard something behind me. I turned around to see Jesus glowing so brightly that I could hardly look at him. He started to move toward me as though

he knew me and wanted to greet me with a hug. But I became extremely frightened and fell to the floor, closing my eyes and curling up into a ball as his light engulfed me. At this moment I awoke from the dream as if trying to escape from the scene. I was scared to death and sweating. But once I was awake, I felt upset with myself for not having the courage and trust to be in his presence. My bedroom seemed unusually dark and empty. I felt so alone and separated that I vowed never to flee again. Even though I prayed intensely, it took me a long time to get back to sleep.

Dreams from the superconscious can be very intense and filled with meaning, symbology, and direct content with everything an individual holds sacred. Without getting into too much interpretation of this dream, we can see how the dreamer's superconscious portrayed him as a ship with twelve engines (spiritual centers, chakras) and how the conscious self was working on getting all twelve engines running properly. Because of this good work and the dreamer's seeking, he received the opportunity to actually meet the one he sought, Jesus. But it was more than he could bear at this time; certainly it prepared him for a future meeting. The dreamer told me he had only experienced the presence of Jesus once before in a dream and in that case he did not directly see him, just felt he was next to him. He was looking forward to a future meeting and hoped he wouldn't be so scared.

Here is another contact dream but with a little less intensity.

I was walking along the lake at an area where the trees hang over the bank, making it difficult to get by. As I got through the trees I was startled to see a

strange man right there in front of me. At first I was
very concerned, but he seemed okay. He hadn't noticed me yet. He was fishing. So I carefully continued to walk past him. As I got closer he turned and
smiled. I smiled back and managed to ask if he was
catching anything. He said, "Yes, but there is one
particular fish I've been trying to catch for a very
long time and I just can't seem to catch her. Will you
help me?" I said I would help him, and then, as
though I was helping I just continued to walk by him
and along the bank. After I had gotten much further
along, I realized I knew who the man was! It was
Jesus. And I knew who the fish was that he wanted
me to help him catch, it was me! When I woke up I
felt very good, even excited and ready to go.

Contact dreams are a passage to the spiritual realm and
the spirit of God that can be traveled while still incarnate.
Be open to this passage to the spirit. Pay attention to your
dreams. Write them down, review them, think about them
and work to understand the information contained in them.
They are a valuable resource and can serve as a doorway to
knowing the deeper levels of the self.

# 13

## Closing Thoughts

IN REVIEWING THE past twenty years of working with the secret teachings and the tools for transformation, and with many different people who are doing the same, I've thought of a few things to share with you that you may find helpful in your journey.

In the beginning of this adventure it is very exciting and rewarding. Your whole life seems to open up in ways you never thought possible. But as time goes on it becomes less exciting and more a matter of doing what you know must be done. The beauty of knowing who we really are is wonderful, but living it daily can be difficult. The disciple John had a very good insight into this experience when he viewed himself eating the "Book of Life" during his revelation: ". . . I took the little book out of the angel's hand, and ate it up; and it was in my mouth sweet as honey: and as soon as I had eaten it, my belly was bitter." (Rev. 10:9) The knowledge of true life is sweet upon first tasting but, as one assimilates it, it can be bitter.

We need to keep a very special tool with us throughout

the journey—*patience*. Without it I don't think any of us can make it. With patience we can continue to live in the physical world while becoming more and more alive to the spiritual one.

Keep a sense of humor, too. I've noticed that we have a tendency to become too serious about spiritual things. Not all of physical life is evil or mundane, and not all of the resurrection is about bearing a cross.

When you aren't sure about where you're going or how well you're doing, *relax*. Becoming uptight, worried, doubtful, skeptical, or depressed is natural and to some degree, healthy; but don't let it drag on too long. Relax. Forget about your own worries and look around for someone else to help for a while. Become concerned about their problems and do what you can to help them. Focusing less on yourself and more on helping others can do wonders for your own mental state.

When things become too much for you, lighten the demands you're placing on yourself. Balance out your life between heavy and light, serious and funny, work and play, purposefulness and nonsense. Take a long, slow walk with a child or learn a new song to sing in the shower or a new joke to share with some friends.

Another old saying that has helped me with patience and staying relaxed yet focused on what I know must be done is, "Be content, but never satisfied." There's a certain energy to contentment that is needed if we are to succeed without wasting ourselves, whereas satisfaction implies an acceptance of what is. We need to keep reaching beyond our present levels if we are to regain our greater state, but do so with a patient, contented energy.

Another problem along the path is the fear of evil. If we spent half as much time *seeking* the light as we do worrying about what the darkness is up to, we'd be there by now! Certainly one should judge the forces that one is aligned with, and evil should be overcome, but all of the path is not wrestling with evil; much of it is becoming more and more familiar with the Light.

Don't be swayed by others or ideas of "how you're supposed to do it." Feel it out for yourself with your deeper self. Remember, "God will teach them directly." Take him up on this promise.

The deeper self is so naturally you that we often miss it and build an elaborate image of some angellike figure to which we can't completely relate. The deeper self sees with the same eyes, hears with the same ears, and lives in the same body. *It is you*, and more than just you as you normally think of yourself. But, it is *you*. It's the better you.

We are spirits in bodies for a time. Our purpose for being is companionship with the Creator of the entire universe. The events we experience in our lives today are the result of our souls' thoughts, actions, and choices in the past. The sorrows, disappointments, limitations, and pain we experience are opportunities to make new and wiser decisions that will change all our tomorrows. Seek and you shall find, ask and it will be shown to you, knock and the door shall be opened *for you*. It is your birthright, your purpose, your destiny to fulfill.

# APPENDIX ONE

# About Edgar Cayce

EDGAR CAYCE WAS born on a farm near Hopkinsville, Kentucky, on March 18, 1877. As a child he displayed unusual powers of perception. At the age of six he told his parents that he could see and talk with "visions," sometimes of relatives who had recently died. He could also sleep with his head on his schoolbooks and awake with a photographic memory of their contents. However, after completing seventh grade he left school to find his place in the world. When he was twenty-one, he developed a paralysis of the throat muscles that caused him to lose his voice. When doctors were unable to find a physical cause for this condition, Edgar Cayce asked a friend to help him reenter the same kind of hypnotic sleep that had enabled him to memorize his schoolbooks as a child. His friend gave him the necessary suggestions, and once he was in his trance state, Edgar spoke clearly and directly to the problem. He recommended some specific medication and manipulative therapy that successfully restored his voice.

Doctors around Hopkinsville and Bowling Green, Kentucky, took advantage of Cayce's unique talent to diagnose their own patients. They soon discovered that all Cayce needed was the name and address of a patient and he could "tune in" telepathically to that individual's mind and body. The patient didn't have to be near Cayce. Wherever they were he could tune in to them.

When one of the young doctors working with Cayce submitted a report on his strange abilities to a clinical research society in Boston, the reactions were amazing. On October 9, 1910, *The New York Times* carried two pages of headlines and pictures. From then on, people from all over the country sought the "sleeping prophet," as he was to become known.

His routine for conducting a trance diagnosis was to recline on a couch, hands folded across his chest, and breathe deeply. Eventually, his eyelids would begin fluttering. This was the signal to the conductor (usually his wife, Gertrude) to make verbal contact with Cayce's subconscious by giving a suggestion. Unless this procedure was timed to synchronize with his fluttering eyelids, Cayce would proceed beyond his trance state and simply fall fast asleep. Once the suggestion was made, Cayce would proceed to describe the patient as if he or she were sitting right next to him, his mind functioning much as an X-ray scanner seeing into every cell of the body. When he was finished, he would say, "Ready for questions." However, in many cases his mind would have already anticipated the patient's questions, answering them during the main session. Eventually, he would say, "We are through for the present," whereupon the conductor would give the suggestion to return to consciousness.

If this procedure was in any way violated, Cayce was in

serious personal danger. On one occasion, he remained in a trance state for three days and actually had been given up for dead by the attending doctors.

At each session a stenographer (usually Gladys Davis Turner, his personal secretary) would record everything Cayce said. Sometimes during a trance session Cayce would even correct the stenographer's spelling. It was as if his mind was in touch with everything around him and beyond.

It was August 10, 1923, before anyone thought to ask the "sleeping" Cayce for insights beyond physical health— questions about life, death, and human destiny. In a small hotel room in Dayton, Ohio, Arthur Lammers asked the first set of philosophical questions that were to lead to an entirely new way of using Cayce's strange abilities. It was during this line of questioning that Cayce first began to talk about reincarnation as if it were as real and natural as a physical body.

Eventually, Edgar Cayce, following advice from his own "readings," as they were now being called, moved to Virginia Beach, Virginia, and set up a hospital where he continued to conduct his "physical readings" for the health of others. But he also continued this new line of readings called "life readings." From 1925 through 1944 he conducted some 2,500 of these life readings, describing the past lives of individuals as casually as if everyone understood reincarnation was a reality. Such subjects as deep-seated fears, mental blocks, vocational talents, innate urges and abilities, marriage difficulties, child training, etc., were examined in the light of what Edgar Cayce called the "karmic patterns" resulting from previous lives spent by the individual's soul on the earth plane.

When he died on January 3, 1945, in Virginia Beach, he left well over 14,000 documented stenographic records of the telepathic-clairvoyant readings he had given for more than 6,000 different people over a period of forty-three years.

The readings constitute one of the largest and most impressive records of psychic perception. Together with their relevant records, correspondence, and reports, they have been cross-indexed under thousands of subject headings and placed at the disposal of psychologists, students, writers, and investigators who still come to examine them. Of course, they are also available to the general public.

A foundation known as the A.R.E. (Association for Research and Enlightenment, Inc., 67th St. & Atlantic Avenue, Virginia Beach, VA 23451) was founded in 1932 to preserve these readings. As an open-membership research society, it continues to index and catalogue the information, initiate investigation and experiments, and conduct conferences, seminars, and lectures. The A.R.E. also has the largest and finest library of parapsychological and metaphysical books in the world. It also maintains a mail-order bookstore with a catalog of over 300 titles of the best books in these areas of human study.

# APPENDIX TWO

# Reincarnation and Christianity

REINCARNATION HAS HAD little, if any, place in mainstream Christianity. However, it was an accepted concept during the time of Christ, shortly after his resurrection, and long before his birth. Furthermore, there is some evidence that the concepts of reincarnation were stricken from the Church theology and even modified in the Bible at the Fifth Ecumenical Congress of Constantinople in A.D. 553. At this congress, the writings of the teachings of many earlier teachers, including Plato, were denounced and expunged from the Church's body of knowledge.

Here are a few examples of these early teachings.

> Know that if you become worse you will go to the worse souls, and if better, to the better souls; and in every succession of life and death you will do and suffer what like must fitly suffer at the hands of like.
> PLATO (582–507 B.C.), *The Republic*

> Every soul . . . comes into this world strengthened by the victories or weakened by the defeats of its

previous life. Its place in this world as a vessel appointed to honor or dishonor is determined by its previous merits or demerits. Its work in this world determines its place in the world which is to follow this.

ORIGEN (A.D. 185–254), *De Principiis*

We were in being long before the foundation of the world; we existed in the eye of God, for it is our destiny to live in Him. We are reasonable creatures of the Divine Word; therefore we have existed from the beginning, for in the beginning was the Word.

ST. CLEMENT OF ALEXANDRIA (A.D. 150–220)

. . . It is absolutely necessary that the soul should be healed and purified, and if this does not take place during its life on earth, it must be accomplished in future lives.

ST. GREGORY (A.D. 257–332)

The messages of Plato, the purest and the most luminous of all philosophy, has at last scattered the darkness of error, and now shines forth mainly in Plotinus, a Platonist so like his master that one would think they lived together, or rather—since so long a period of time separates them—that Plato was born again in Plotinus.

ST. AUGUSTINE (A.D. 354–430)

Beyond the teachings and ideas of these early church fathers, we actually find passages in the Bible that may indicate a knowledge and acceptance of reincarnation. Here are a few examples.

The Lord possessed me in the beginning of his way, before his works of old.
I was set up from everlasting, from the beginning, or ever the earth was.

When there were no depths, I was brought forth; when there were no fountains abounding with water.

Before the mountains were settled, before the hills was I brought forth:

While as yet he had not made the earth, nor the fields, nor the highest part of the dust of the world.

When he prepared the heavens, I was there: when he set a compass upon the face of the depth:

When he established the clouds above: when he strengthened the fountains of the deep:

When he gave to the sea his decree, that the waters should not pass his commandment: when he appointed the fountains of the earth:

Then I was by him, as one brought up with him. . . .

Proverbs 8:22–30

Behold, I will send you Elijah (as called Elias) the prophet, before the coming of the great and dreadful day of the lord.

Malachi 4:5

. . . The angel said unto him, Fear not Zacharias: for thy prayer is heard; and thy wife Elisabeth shall bear thee a son, and thou shalt call his name John.

And thou shalt have joy and gladness; and many shall rejoice at his birth.

For he shall be great in the sight of the Lord, and shall drink neither wine nor strong drink; and he shall be filled with the Holy Ghost, even from his mother's womb.

. . . And he shall go before him *in the spirit and power of Elias*. . . . [italics mine]

Luke 1:13–17

And His disciples asked Him, saying, "Why then say the scribes that Elias (Elijah) must first come?" And Jesus answered and said unto them, "Elias truly shall first come, and restore all things. But I say unto you that Elias is come already, and they knew him

not, but have done unto him whatsoever they liked.
Likewise shall also the Son of Man suffer of them.''
Then the disciples understood that he spake unto them
of John the Baptist.

Matthew 17:9–13


. . . All the prophets and the law prophesied until
John (the Baptist). And if ye will receive it, this is
Elias, which has to come. He that hath ears to hear,
let him hear.

Matthew 11:13–14


And as Jesus passed by, he saw a man which was
blind from his birth. And His disciples asked Him,
saying, ''Master, who did sin, this man or his parents; that he was *born blind?*'' [italics mine]

John 9:1–2


Him that overcometh will I make a pillar in the
temple of the Lord, *and he shall go no more out*.
[italics mine]

Revelation 3:12


Certainly reincarnation is not accepted as a teaching of
Christianity, but there is evidence that it was at one time as
well understood by Christians as by Hindus and Buddhists.

# Recommended Reading

Bolduc, Henry. *The Journey Within: Past-Life Regression & Channeling*. Virginia Beach, VA: Inner Vision Publishing.

Bro, Harmon, Ph.D. *Edgar Cayce on Dreams*. New York: Warner Books.

Cerminara, Gina, Ph.D. *Many Mansions: The Edgar Cayce Story on Reincarnation*. Virginia Beach, VA: A.R.E. Press.

Church, W. H. *Many Happy Returns: The Lives of Edgar Cayce*. San Francisco: Harper & Row.

Furst, Jeffery. *Edgar Cayce's Story of Jesus*. Virginia Beach, VA: A.R.E. Press.

Reed, Henry, Ph.D. *Getting Help from Your Dreams*. Virginia Beach, VA: Inner Vision Publishing.

Sanderfur, Glenn. *Lives of the Master*. Virginia Beach, VA: A.R.E. Press.

Sechrist, Elsie. *Dreams: Your Magic Mirror*. New York: Warner Books.

Sechrist, Elsie. *Meditation: Gateway to Light*. Virginia Beach, VA: A.R.E. Press.

Shelley, Violet. *Reincarnation Unnecessary*. Virginia Beach, VA: A.R.E. Press.

Smith, A. Robert. *Hugh Lynn Cayce: About My Father's Business*. Virginia Beach, VA: Donning Co.

Sparrow, G. Scott, Ph.D. *Lucid Dreaming: Dawning of the Clear Light*. Virginia Beach, VA: A.R.E. Press.

Sparrow, Lynn. *Reincarnation: Claiming Your Past, Creating Your Future*. San Francisco: Harper & Row.

Sugrue, Thomas. *There is a River: The Story of Edgar Cayce*. Virginia Beach, VA: A.R.E. Press.

Thurston, Mark, Ph.D. *The Inner Power of Silence: A Universal Way of Meditation*. Virginia Beach, VA: Inner Vision Publishing.

Wilhelm, Richard, trans. *The Secret of the Golden Flower*. New York: Harcourt Brace & Jovanovich.

# About the Author

John Van Auken has spent much of his life seeking answers to our greatest questions. He has been with A.R.E., the Edgar Cayce organization, for nineteen years and is widely known through his lectures and books. This book is an outgrowth of his passion for understanding.

He invites anyone interested in learning about workshops or other related activities to write him in care of his publisher, Ballantine Books, 201 E. 50th St., New York, NY 10022.

# Go Beyond
# the Limits of
# Mind and Body...